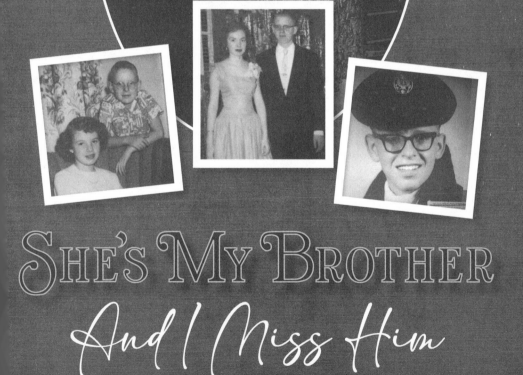

She's My Brother

And I Miss Him

SHIRLEYANNE THOM

SHE'S MY BROTHER
And I Miss Him

SHIRLEYANNE THOM

Published by EDK Books and
Distributed by EDK Distribution, LLC
edkbookdistribution.com
edkbooksanddistribution@gmail.com
(206) 227-8179

She's My Brother . . . And I Miss Him

Copyright © 2021 by Shirleyanne Thom

10 9 8 7 6 5 4 3 2 1

Printed in the United States of America

ISBN 978-1-7339618-8-2

Editor: Barbara Kindness

Design: Julie K. Lee

ACKNOWLEDGMENTS

I'd like to thank the following persons who offered their support to Gene as he went through his transition: our current family, particularly cousins Texanna Casey Thompson and Jaqi Thompson, as well as our bluegrass friends, Laurel Bliss, Cliff Perry, and Mary Fleischman. Gene was particularly encouraged by your support.

CONTENTS

FOREWORD

This is the story of a sister and brother who were very close—in age, attitude, and shared activities. Then, one day, the brother nearly died ... and on that very day, a new family truth began to emerge. Shirleyanne and Gene had to examine all they thought they knew about each other. They had to learn to live with a new understanding of their personal realities.

I am Shirleyanne, the sister, who believed I had a brother named Gene. In the weeks following his near-death, I learned that Gene had always thought of himself as my sister. He revealed to me that he was a cross-dresser. I learned this in my home, where he was recuperating from his hospital stay.

He was fifty-three years old, and I was fifty-four. That's a long time for two people to live a lie; for two siblings who had presumed they were close. But we weren't the only ones living the lie. Our parents had insisted that Gene's cross-dressing remain a secret. Family secrets, unfortunately, are all too common ... and hurtful.

Because I fancy myself to be tolerant of personal choices, I didn't think there would be a complicated transition in my thought processes ... if my brother chose to wear a dress, it wasn't a big deal. In fact, the day after he revealed his florid, silky self to me, we went shopping together, and I bought him a new dress. We both were exhilarated that this long-held family secret was finally revealed. What a fun day it was!

Gene was relieved by my immediate acceptance. He finally had a place where he could be himself in all his feminine finery. But it wasn't long before the nature and frequency of our time together changed drastically. He began to come to my home every weekend to push his personal agenda of showing me all his underwear and silky dresses. Rather than set limits on how he shared his wardrobe, and how much time and space he was taking from me, I attempted to bury the resentment that was creeping into my feelings for him.

Gene had lived a lonely, solitary life inside his protected personal identity. I didn't want to send him back into his closet. But resentment doesn't bury easily. We had a difficult two years that ended one Sunday afternoon.

"You've changed," he said, as he packed up his belongings and left in a huff. He left me standing by myself in the doorway to my bedroom, wondering when, or if, I would see him again.

I've changed?!? I thought to myself, incredulously. And you haven't?!? Fine. You've just given me my life back. But I soon realized that this would mean a life without my brother. I couldn't let it end like that.

Fortunately, Gene and I were part of a strong, loving family, so we saw each other at birthday parties and holiday gatherings. A couple of years after our abrupt estrangement, I called him at work and invited him to a baseball game. He accepted my invitation. I vowed to myself that I would find a way for us to see each other again, but with an understanding of certain limitations.

Gene accepted the limitations, but he wanted his story told. We recorded many hours of conversations so I could understand who he was, then share my understanding with others. This book is our story. It includes his confessions and the effects of his disclosures as they unfolded. I did not edit the words he spoke; they are as he expressed them. My thoughts are my own and written as they came to me, at the time they appeared in my mind. They too are unedited. Parts of this book could be a tough read.

I'm not sure I understand the complexities of cross-dressing, but I understand more than I did. I am sharing our story because I hope our personal journey will bring about a greater appreciation for the vastness and varieties of the human race. We are all a part of it, and we are worth the effort it will take for us humans to learn to live better together.

LIMERICK

There once was a young man named Gene
Who loved to add spice to the scene
By spending the day
Wearing pink lingerie
'Neath a dress that was fit for a queen.

Gene Wilson

PART ONE

Chapter One

SHOUTS FROM STRANGERS
My Brother Is Dying

"He's failing! He's failing!"

The words are hurling across the room, striking my ears. I think they mean my brother is dying, but I'm not sure. The words are coming from strangers in my living room. If Gene were dying this close to me, I think I'd feel it, but I don't feel anything. My senses are untouched. The words are piercing my eardrums and nothing more. My heart is not pounding, my brain is not reeling. My brother is *not* dying.

The activity in my living room contradicts my confidence. Two firemen are across the room frantically applying their resuscitating magic to the man on the couch. The magic doesn't appear to be working. They're losing him. The man on the couch is dying. The man on the couch is my brother.

I'm passively watching the action as if a veil has dropped, separating me from the life-and-death drama taking place just a few feet away from me. It was only a little while ago that we returned to my condo from Husky Stadium, where the University of Washington football team racked up their third victory of the season. Gene was planning to spend the night at my place so he could drive me to the airport tomorrow morning.

Tomorrow is my birthday and I'm flying to California to meet my daughter Rebecca; her husband, Mark; and their three kids, my grandkids, at Disneyland. They're already on the road, driving the twenty-two hours it takes to get from Seattle to Disneyland. I love them to pieces, but twenty-two hours in a car with three kids is not my definition of some place I want to be. It's the close quarters of the car that bothers me, not the kids themselves. Sharing Disneyland with them is a wonderful place to be. Sailing through the lusty rivers of the Pirates of the Caribbean and whirling around and around in giant Alice in Wonderland teacups in the company of my succeeding generations is my ultimate anti-aging birthday present. I was eagerly anticipating the sensations of a Disneyland time warp. But that's not going to happen, is it?

Five minutes after we arrived at my condo after the football game, Gene walked toward me from the bathroom and said, "I'm having trouble breathing."

I hear an edge of distress in his voice.

"Shall I dial 9-1-1?" I ask.

"Yeah, I think so," he responds quietly.

It's time to move. I'm on the phone.

"My brother is having trouble breathing … he's fifty-two … we just got back from the Huskies game and … well, yes. He was walking kind of slow on the way to the car … 2415 Western Avenue, Number 226 …"

"We're on our way," I hear on the other end of the line.

I hang up the phone and turn toward Gene. He's shuffled his way across the room and dropped himself onto the edge of the couch, leaning straight back with his legs extending to the floor like a stiff board. His arms are lying alongside his torso with his hands dangling over the seat cushions. His face is looking up at the ceiling; his mouth is open. I walk toward him, hesitant, not knowing what to do. I'm feeling useless. 9-1-1 better hurry. His skin is turning a purplish-blue color. He hasn't stopped breathing. He's fighting to breathe … sounds juicy, like gurgling. Should I try CPR? I don't know.

I'm afraid that whatever I do will interfere with what he's trying to do on his own, which is trying to breathe. His color is changing again. I now know what they mean when they say people turn black. I couldn't imagine it before, but now I see it. Gene is turning black. The panic of pending death comes quickly.

I try talking to him. "Hang on, Gene … they'll be here any minute. Come on. Keep it going …"

He nods. Yes! He's going to be okay.

Oh God. His eyes just rolled back. "Gene!"

He's not responding. Damn it! Where the hell are they? … "GENE!"

WHAM! The door bursts open. Three medics come crashing through the doorway. They run right over to Gene. "Get the mask on him! We gotta get a vein. Try here …"

I hear clothing being ripped.

"I can't get to him! Let's move some of this furniture."

"He's a big fella … Let's lay him down … We need help …"

"This is Jim at 2415 Western Avenue, number 226. Send us reinforcement. We have a serious situation …"

The fireman turns to me. "Ma'am, your brother is very, very sick …"

"I know."

I step back, giving them more room to maneuver. I watch them and listen closely to what they're saying, trying to get a feel for how sick he is.

Drug paraphernalia is flying around the room. The medics are moving fast, with well-practiced authority. When you watch something like this on TV, you don't get a sense of how powerful the actions are. The three men fill the room with their efforts.

C'mon, Gene. Fight! I'm sending him messages from my heart, but I don't feel his heart responding.

They're putting an oxygen mask over his nose and mouth, and they're hovering over him—working, talking, crinkling paper, tossing hypodermic syringes, trying to find a viable vein, trying to get any kind of response from their patient—while their patient's sister is watching from a few feet away. I'm taking it all in as I keep sending my brother silent, ineffective messages, desperately hoping to touch his innate will to live. Gene just lies there. What does he know? What does he feel?

Does he know there are people in this room he's never met, working hard to save his life? Does he know I'm here, willing his heart to try harder? Is he aware of anything that's going on? Does he know he's supposed to help us? Gene, you have to help us. You must survive this!

• • • • •

If you leave me tonight, I am alone. Dad's long gone, more than thirty years. Mom's gone too, more than a decade. If you leave, I'm all that's left of our little family of four. Just one person. What kind of family is that?

Gene and I each live alone. He lives in Bellingham, Washington, and I live in Seattle, ninety miles south. Although Gene has had relationships with women, he never married. He seems to prefer solitude to the daily chit chat of a live-in partner. It took me two marriages to figure out I like living alone. I'm not good at the dailies. At least I have kids from my first marriage and my kids have kids, my grandkids, to show for my marital misadventures. And I have Gene. My brother Gene is my life partner.

But Gene is no recluse and neither am I. We have a large extended family, and Gene is an integral part of all that we do as a family. Kids love him, just like they love any quiet person who gives them a nod and a poke in the ribs, and does irreverent things at unexpected moments. Who else but an Uncle Gene would present a Whoopee cushion to a shy seven-year-old boy, and demonstrate how it works at the dinner table?

Outside the family, Gene is well-known for his avocations. He deeply believes in the preservation of our American culture. For his radio shows at the college stations in Bellingham and Seattle, he uses his private music collection and wry presentation skills to introduce new generations to our musical heritage and to satisfy old-timers' hankerings for blue grass and mountain folk tunes. And despite his natural reticence to call attention to himself, he'll pick up his banjo and play a few songs for an audience of family, friends, and festivals whenever there's a whiff of music in the air.

Gene is also a lifelong, dyed-in-the-wool baseball fan. A few years back he decided his community needed more exposure to the Seattle Mariners farm team, which was located in Bellingham. He approached a local radio station with the notion that they should broadcast the games.

"Who'll do the play-by-play?" they asked.

"I will," he said. And he did.

Gene has always done what he's wanted to do, quietly and with confidence. In his own self-made way, he has become an important slice of Americana. I know that with his mind, his abilities, and his talents, he could have cut a wide swath in public notoriety. He chose instead to affect the people around him by contributing a small point of difference into the lives of his family and his community. He has instilled in all who know him a basic value for the simple life. With Gene in our lives, we have been able to eventually sort through the bull shit and uncover the basic roots to our own self-fulfillment. He keeps us grounded in a harmonious reality.

BAM! The invisible veil lifts. Three more people burst into the condo, knocking me out of my sentimental reverie. They're dragging a gurney with them.

"We gotta get him off the couch. We need access to all sides …"

"Oh, he's a big fella!"

"I can't find a vein!"

"We've got to get the medicine in him ..."

"Here. Let me try ..."

"Is he on any medication, ma'am? Does he have a doctor?"

"I don't know. I'll call a friend."

"Cliff, we're having a medical emergency here. It's Gene. Medics are working on him. I'm not sure how it's going to turn out. Do you know if he has a doctor in Bellingham? ... Would you call Laurel and see if she knows? I may need you tonight ..."

More shouts from across the room.

"He's failing! ... We're losing him!"

"Gotta go. Bye, Cliff. Call me back."

"We have to get him to the hospital ..."

"This is Aaron in Medic One. We're bringing one in ... male ... fifty-two ... congestive heart failure ... pulmonary cause ... having trouble accessing his veins ... we're on our way ... about eight minutes ..."

"Ma'am, we're taking your brother to Harborview. It's the best place for him to be. It's the only place for him to be right now..."

"Let's get him on the gurney ... Oh, he is big. Come on ... lift!"

"Can I ride with you?" I ask, almost as an afterthought.

"'fraid not, ma'am."

They're gone. The phone rings.

"Hi, Shirleyanne. This is Laurel. I don't know of any doctor that Gene goes to. The only time he's ever gone to a doctor that I know of is when he broke his elbow last year. That was Dr. Mason. How's it going?"

"They just left for Harborview. I'll keep you posted."

I have to make sure I've got everything covered ... what about insurance? Okay ... think. His pants are on the floor. I'll check his wallet. Yes ... yes. There's his insurance card. I'll take the whole wallet with me. What else? Call Shannon (my other daughter) ... done. Call Texie (cousin) ... done. And ... Geez! I gotta call the motel at Disneyland. Where's the itinerary? Over there ... alongside my suitcase.

I'm calling Disneyland. How weird is that? They're not in. I leave a message.

Let's see. Anything else? Gotta get going. Don't think I'll drive. I'm OK, I think, but why chance it. I'll call a cab.

"Emergency to Harborview. Please ... quickly ... 2415 Western Avenue. I'll be waiting outside. How long? ... good. Thanks."

Grab ditty bag from my suitcase ... address book ... don't know how long I'll be. I'm outta here.

We pull up to the Emergency entrance. Gene is somewhere inside that building. An hour ago, Gene and I were driving home together from a football game, part of a fall tradition, part of a lifetime of shared traditions between us. Now we are arriving at this place in separate vehicles. Is this the start of our ultimate separation? I am closer to Gene than to any other person on this earth. He's my brother. He's my best friend. How can he leave me?

I pay the cab driver and walk toward the double doors that lead to the emergency room, not knowing what is waiting inside.

What's going to happen to us?

Chapter Two

AN UNEXPECTED GUEST
My sister arrives

It's Friday night … finally.

I'm almost home after another week of working the media sales hell.

Gene is staying with me. The diagnosis was congestive heart failure. It's a scary, sometimes fatal condition that comes with no warning. The lungs fill up with water, or whatever it is called, and they can't pump blood into the heart to force it to pump the life blood to the places it needs to go. The victim suddenly has trouble breathing, and without immediate medical help, he or she soon can't breathe at all. Life on earth is over.

For a few minutes, less than two weeks ago, I thought I'd lost my brother. The fact that I live close to a fire station probably saved his life. Thanks to the quick actions of firemen and, later, the hospital ER staff, he's alive and recuperating at my place. Here he is close to the doctors at the hospital, and I can keep an eye on him until the intensity of his recovery settles into a self-maintenance routine.

It doesn't take a lot from me to take care of him. I give him a place to stay and show up every night. That's what families do. No discussions needed. Just show up and be available. And I'm more than ready to show up tonight. The work week is over.

My work as a media sales manager is a stressful career choice that has me interfacing with relentless, egocentric people fifty hours a week. About three o'clock every Friday afternoon, my brain leaves work and begins to lock onto the gratification that accompanies the defining edge of a Jack Daniels on the rocks. I picture myself hunkering down on my sofa, at home by myself, sipping the evening away. No plans, no people, no stress.

Tonight will be different because I won't be alone, but it's Friday night and I'm ready to begin a quiet weekend with my brother.

• • • • •

It's almost six o'clock as I back into the front hall of my condo, pushing the door open with my butt. I'm holding a small bag of groceries with my left hand; my left arm is pressing the evening newspaper against my side. My right hand is carrying the obligatory briefcase, a dead weight I intend to throw into the coat closet, where it'll stay until Monday morning. I don't know why I bother carrying that thing home with me. It's a dreadful reminder that weekends are but temporary respites.

Setting the groceries down in the kitchen, I feel an unexpected presence nearby. My weekend meltdown is delayed as a twinge of irritation runs through my body. I don't like having the unexpected intrude into what is meant to be my down time. It's probably a friend of Gene who's dropped by to see how he's doing.

Damn! I didn't figure I'd be having extra company tonight. I listen, hoping to identify the intruder before the introduction takes place. There are no voices, only a few sounds of movement. That's odd. Maybe it's nothing. I put away the groceries and head toward the living room.

Wishful thinking that it would be nothing. There definitely is a presence, and … Oh … my … God! There it is, standing in the hall just a few feet away from me. I stop and stare at this vision in her flowered print dress, with black fishnet stockings covering her legs, and a long pearl necklace hanging across her bosom. Nothing even close to a coherent thought registers in my mind. My brain has ceased to function. I'm locked into a stunned silence. She speaks first.

"We need to talk," she says.

Damn right, I'm thinking.

Without comment, I follow her into the living room—my living room. I don't recall inviting her into my living room this Friday evening. She sits herself down on the black sofa against the wall, the same black sofa that held my brother close to death only a couple of weeks ago. The same black sofa Mr. Jack Rocks and I expected to occupy by ourselves tonight. But she got there first.

I sit on the upholstered chair across the room from her and look above her head, focusing my eyes on the vagrant lines of the Miró aquatints hanging on the wall behind her. My focus wavers when I realize she's looking at me, waiting for some indication from me that our talk can begin. Slowly, I redirect my eyes to her and give her the go-ahead nod she's been waiting for.

She raises her head just a little, hunches her shoulders slightly, and takes in a breath. Then gesturing, she delicately runs her hands down the front of her flowered dress and across her lap. She poses as if to speak. Deliberately, she tucks her skirt under her knees in lady-like fashion and looks at me. Then she quietly introduces herself.

"This is who I am," she says.

I don't know who the 'who' is she's referring to, and I don't particularly care to know. I expected to spend a quiet weekend with my brother. Where the hell is he? I reach inside myself to find a more appropriate response that will display my usual public calm.

"This is who you are … sometimes? … or all the time?" I ask.

"This is the real me," she replies. "This is how I prefer to dress. This is how I dress when I'm alone."

"And this is how you'd like to dress when you're with me?" I ask cautiously.

"Yes," is her quiet response.

"How long have you preferred to dress this way?" I ask.

"Since I was four," she says.

"That wasn't yesterday," is my stupid reply.

I realize I'm sounding like an idiot, but it's buying me time while I try to figure out what this uninvited appearance means. I feel an instant loss of history. Since she, or is it he, was four? This rayon, flower-printed floozy has been in my life since she was four, since I was five?!? No-no-no-no. She wasn't wearing flower-printed dresses when she was four. What was she wearing? And who the hell is she?

This is very confusing. But it's not so confusing that I don't understand my life is about to change, starting when I was five years old. Not possible. How can life begin to change a half-century ago?

This person, this life-changing intruder, has dutifully paused again, waiting for my blank stare to focus back to the moment. I gather my internal resources and center my attention on her.

"Four? When we were living in that little house on 48th Avenue?" I'm trying to form a mental picture of where it was that we first met.

"Yeah," she says. "They say things like this are a choice, but how does a four-year-old boy make a choice like this? He doesn't know anything about a sexual preference; he just knows how he feels. And since I was four, I've had a feeling that I wanted to dress like this."

"And what is this …uh …feeling?" I ask.

"It's something I feel a need to do, and it just builds up and builds up, until I have to do it," she responds.

"And you've felt this way since you were four?" I'm repeating myself.

"Yeah."

"Every day?"

"Yeah."

His "yeahs" are starting to irritate me. I deserve complete sentences with more forthright explanations.

"And … have you always followed through with this feeling?"

"Yeah …whenever I could."

"Did Mom and Dad know?" This seems important to me.

"Yeah," he says again.

"When did they know?" I ask. I don't know why it's important to me, but it is.

"Well, Mom caught me when I was four—when I put on your panties."

"When you put on my pan… What did she do?" I can't even imagine her reaction.

"She made me wear them in front of our relatives—they were visiting from Oregon at the time."

"So, Dad knew then too." It suddenly hits me. They all knew.

"Yeah, I guess. He was there."

"All these years, you and Mom and Dad knew and I didn't. That's disheartening."

"You were there too." There is a tone of accusation in his voice.

"I don't remember seeing you in my panties. I do remember, one time, Mom stood you up on a chair in front of the relatives and you didn't have any clothes on. They all laughed at you. I didn't understand what was going on. That had to have been a terrible experience. Why didn't you ever say anything to me about it?"

"Mom didn't want me to say anything, and I didn't want to burden you. I thought you'd be disappointed, and I didn't want to face that."

I feel a rush of sadness for him. How terribly hard it must have been to keep this to himself for so many years. But … wait a minute. He could have told me. I'm his sister and his friend. He should have told me. I'm more than a little annoyed. Why didn't he share this with me? So many years of being unnecessarily alone. Why didn't he share!

"What you're saying doesn't make sense, Gene. Why would I be disappointed in you? Why would I care about what you wear?"

"It's not how men are supposed to dress," he says.

"Like 'supposed to' carries a lot of weight with me," I respond, with more than a twinge of irritation. "You should know that kind of thing doesn't matter to me."

Now that I'm adjusting to this Friday night surprise, I'm pissed off. The APB that occurred two weekends ago couldn't be helped. One expects to respond appropriately to a life-threatening emergency. But this is no emergency. This is a planned sabotage, dumped in my lap when he knows I'm emotionally vulnerable. I'm glad Gene finally felt he could reveal his feminine inclinations to me, but his timing seams manipulative. I continue with my vexed response.

"Since you've managed to keep this secret from me for fifty years, give or take a few months, why are you choosing to tell me this now? Does it have something to do with what happened here a couple of weeks ago?"

"Probably," he says, ignoring my sarcasm. "I wear women's panties. When I woke up in the hospital, I didn't have them on. I thought you might have seen something."

"Why would I have seen something?"

"I didn't know what went on after I passed out. But I knew I was wearing panties, and when I woke up at the hospital, I wasn't wearing anything but the hospital gown. Someone knew I was wearing panties because somebody took them off of me. I thought you probably did, and I figured maybe this was the catalyst I needed to get this whole thing out in the open. The main thing on my mind from then on was how to get the dialogue started.

"I was hoping, because I'm a coward, that seeing the panties would make you ask about them. Then I wouldn't have to start the dialogue myself. When you brought me my clothes, they were in the cellophane bag the hospital gave you and the panties were showing, you know, right through the cellophane. I don't know how you couldn't have seen them. You took the bag home and you brought it back when I was released. I wondered why you brought it back. How come you didn't look in my overnight bag?"

"I did look," I say. "The hospital gave me your clothes in the bag and I set it down in the den and added your pants to it. I didn't look in the bag. Your pants probably covered your underwear. When it was time to bring you home, I started to unzip your suitcase and I saw what looked like a flowered dress and I said to myself, 'can't wear that'. I didn't think any more about it. I just closed the suitcase and thought, well, I guess he'll have to wear the clothes in the bag. I didn't notice that your pants were ripped all the way down both legs.

"I don't know why I thought it was so funny when you came out of the bathroom in the hospital wearing cords with the sides split open and the pants legs flapping. I couldn't help but laugh. The pants looked goofy enough, but what was so hilarious was the look on your face. You were so nonplussed about it, as if you always wore pants that looked like that. And you stood there looking at me like you couldn't see what the hell was so damn funny, which made it even funnier."

I'm laughing out loud now, as I recall the scene.

"So, you *did* know," he says.

He's not laughing with me. My nervous rambling failed to distract him from the fact that I did see a dress in his suitcase. I hadn't remembered it until he just brought it up. Why not? Was it denial?

"Well, you know," I concede, "nothing registered in my mind that the dress was important. I flashed back to when you were about fifteen and Mom caught you in one of my dresses. I figured it was some teenage hormonal thing at the time and I never thought about it again. Then, when I saw the dress in your suitcase, I thought you still liked to wear a dress once in a while. It wasn't a big deal to me. I don't worry about people's fetishes. I believe that, as long as it doesn't hurt anybody, people should have personal freedom of expression. That's why all the nuts in the world are drawn to me … oops. Sorry."

Fortunately, he overlooks that slip of the tongue. I recover quickly. "Did it disappoint you that I didn't say anything?"

"No," he says. "It just made it harder for me. It put the onus back on me to bring it up, which is where it belonged in the first place.

"I knew I was going to stay in Seattle for a while, so I needed to go back to Bellingham to get some more clothes. I waited until I was sure it would be okay for me to drive. That was Tuesday.

"When I got back to Seattle, that night I put on panties and a T-shirt to sleep in, and I left the door open and decided to sleep on top of the covers, thinking you would come in, in the morning, to check on me. But you didn't do that, so my plan didn't work.

"Wednesday night, I figured maybe you couldn't tell they were panties with the T-shirt half-covering them, so I put on my slip and slept on top of the covers again. I thought for sure you'd see it. But that didn't work either."

I laugh. "All these scenarios were going on inside your head and I was blissfully unaware. If I saw the door open, I wouldn't go near the room for fear of invading your privacy."

"Then today," he continues, "you were supposed to come back on your lunch hour to bring me the garage beeper so I could get out and go to Bellingham to pick up my paycheck. When I got up, I dressed up completely in nylons and everything, and at ten o'clock I was in the kitchen when I heard your key in the door. It seemed like I agonized a long time, trying to decide … shall I do this now, or … and then I thought you might have someone with you. So, I made a mad dash to get back in the den and jumped under the covers. Again, I thought for sure you would have seen me at least go around the corner, but you didn't."

"Actually," I interrupt, "I did see a blur leaping into the den. I figured you weren't dressed yet, so I elected not to say anything."

"It was at that moment," Gene says, "I decided today would be the day—the 11th of October, the day that will become my real birthday.

"After you left, I changed back into men's clothes and drove to Bellingham. All the way back, it was on my mind that I was going to do this tonight. I was planning what I was going to say. I thought the first thing would be to apologize for putting you in that position, and hopefully I would get the rest of it off my chest before you threw me out."

"You thought I'd throw you out?"

"I was scared shitless. I almost chickened out. But I decided I had to do it, and the only way was to get into a dress and wait until it was too late, and you were already here, and there wouldn't be anything I could do about it. I waited in the den until I was sure you weren't bringing anyone home with you. And from then on, I was so nervous and scared I don't remember what I was thinking."

"I can't believe you thought I'd throw you out."

"Well, see, this type of thing … people's reactions are so irrational. And a lot of people … who are reasonable people … you never know what they'll do …."

I look at Gene and try to imagine what these past few days have been like for him, all the plotting going on in his mind, not knowing how this would turn out. And I never noticed that anything was going on. He was scattering clues all over the place, and I was clueless. He had to do this brave thing without any help from me. It was a huge risk on his part. My self-pity is waning.

"So now that you know I know, what's going to happen?" I ask.

"You'll probably see a lot more of me now, more than you want, because now I have two places to wear my 'real' clothes."

That's something to think about. Right now, I see my brother about as much as I want to. Along with my privacy fetish comes a real need for solitude and space.

We talk for a while longer and suddenly I'm very tired. It's been a long week and I didn't get to relax with my Jack. We haven't had dinner, but I'm not hungry. One glass of Jack will have to do. I'm physically and emotionally exhausted. Where's the pillow? He or she can get his or her own dinner.

"Gene, I'm tired. I think I want to sleep on this. I'm glad you finally told me. I wish you'd told me sooner, but you did tell me, so I won't belabor that. We'll talk more in the morning. And don't run off. I'm not going to throw you out. My 'throw-the-bum-out' threshold is a lot higher than hearing this new information."

I leave him there in the living room as I settle into my bed to consider the evening's revelations. First, I have to acknowledge his courage. He took this on, coming right after a life-threatening experience that may yield significant health burdens. In addition to the heart problems, Type 2 diabetes was diagnosed.

Second, I understand why he's telling me now. He got a close look into the face of his mortality, and as he said, it posed the perfect opportunity for him to come out. If he's going to get to live any part of his life as the person he really is, he has to go for it now.

Third, I don't see how his coming out will significantly change our relationship, once I get used to the new landscape. Gene has been wearing women's clothing behind my back nearly all of our lives, and our relationship has been strong. I don't see how his wearing dresses in front of me will alter what we have.

But there is a rub to this exploratory game I'm playing with myself. With Gene being the exception, I've always felt there was something different about me; something that kept me from establishing a level of intimacy that other people seem to have.

Mom and Dad played the "let's keep Shirleyanne in the dark" game for all my growing up years. Gene went along with it because they told him to. Their little club was exclusive, excluding me. No wonder I feel like an outsider. Gene has handed me an excuse as well as someone to blame for my emotional short-comings. This is quite handy. I've been given the chance to use the ultimate "it's not my fault" cop-out.

Nope. Can't do it. This isn't about me. This situation, or whatever one wants to call it, needs to have a happy ending. There's been too much deprivation for way too long.

My brother doesn't deserve a lifetime of feeling he has to hide a personal trait that harms no one. I have to get over myself and see what I can do to help Gene live at least some of his personal reality. I couldn't bear living with his kind of loneliness. Thank God there's time left to bring about a new level of social inclusion, for both of us.

Now that I've got my head on straight, I can go to sleep. Tomorrow begins a new relationship with my brother . . . or is it my sister?

Chapter Three

HER FIRST ARRIVAL
At age four

It was a good sleep. I hear Gene moving around in the living room. I wonder what he's wearing. Assorted thoughts are running through my head as I prepare for this new day. What's next?

Ah! There she is again … another flowered dress. He does like the flowered look. He? She? Is he a she, or is she a he? Or … is she still a he but with she tendencies? It may take a while for me to get this gender thing right. I think I'll fix us some breakfast before we talk. I nod at Gene and head for the kitchen.

After we've eaten breakfast and resumed our Friday night positions on the chair and sofa, I say, "Okay Gene, can we go back to when you were four and you had this urge to wear my clothes? I know you told me about it last night but I'm a little fuzzy on the details."

He looks relieved, perhaps because he wondered what I'd say or do on this second day of disclosure. He begins. "My first foray into cross-dressing took place when I was four. Even at that age, for quite some time when I was by myself, I would find myself imagining what it would be like to do whatever I was doing, as a girl. In those days, being a girl meant wearing dresses. When I would see you, my sister, wearing a pretty dress, I wished I could wear a dress too.

"At the time, we lived in a small house and we shared a bedroom. Your bed was on one side of the room and mine was on the other side, with a chest of drawers in between the beds. We shared the chest of drawers.

"I had my bath first that night, and you were in having your bath. I was in the bedroom by myself and I just had this urge to put on a pair of your panties. You were out of the room, so I decided to risk it. I took a pair of your panties out of the chest of drawers and put them on. I don't know if you remember, but the panties at that time were a sort of silky fabric, with horizontal stripes of a two-toned dusty pink color. You know, when you go to a baseball game you notice they mow the grass one way, then they mow it the other way, and it produces a striped effect. These panties were like that. You wore that kind for quite a few years."

"I remember the fabric." (Who cares about the fabric? I want to get on to the crux of the experience.) "So, you had the urge to put on my panties. Why? How did that come about? Were you just drawn to the drawer?"

"Yeah," he says. "And when I put the panties on, I was immediately overcome by a wonderful feeling of joy. It just felt so right.

"As good as it felt, however, I knew even then that boys were not supposed to have such feelings, much less act on them. So, I took the panties off and put them back in the drawer, and got into bed.

"Then you came back after your bath and got into bed too. And, you know how little kids, if they can't see your eyes, they think you can't see them? Well, the chest of drawers was between us and stupid me, figuring that since I couldn't see your eyes, you couldn't see me either. I got out of bed, got the panties out, and put them on again."

"Why?" I ask.

"It just felt right to do it. And you saw me, of course. You were probably wondering what the fuck was going on, and you called Mom and she came into the room."

"I doubt that word entered my brain at such a tender age. I wonder why I called her in."

Ignoring my response, Gene restates his position. "As I said, you were probably wondering what the fuck was going on here. I mean, you must have been thrown for a loop. It didn't bother me that you called her. It made perfectly good sense to me. Even though I was scared, I didn't blame you."

"I don't remember much about it," I say. "But you knew you shouldn't be wearing my panties, and I guess I knew you shouldn't be wearing them. How did we know that? How old were we, again?"

"I was four, and you were five. Old enough to have a feel for what would fly and what wouldn't."

"What did I do?" I ask. "Did I just holler, 'Mom, come in here and see what Gene is doing?'"

"I don't remember exactly what you said. An aunt and uncle were visiting at the time. What Mom did was pick me up out of bed and carry me, clad only in your panties, into the living room. She showed me off to the relatives and Dad, who was also in the living room. They were all amused, but seemed less interested in my wearing girls' undies than the fact that, at the tender age of four, I had an erection going on. I think they were more impressed with that than anything."

I chuckle at that. "An erection on a four-year-old would be impressive to any observer.

"As I said last night, I remember your being almost naked in front of every-body, but I didn't remember what led up to it. All I remember is her carrying you into the living room. There was a floor furnace in the room and she put you on a chair above that, I thought, to keep you warm.

"I don't remember the panties. But now that you bring it up, I guess I do recall the erection. Of course, I didn't know what it was, or why it was there, and I didn't care. I thought she was trying to embarrass you for some reason, by showing what your 'goob,' as she called it, was doing, and I know I didn't like her doing that. They were all laughing and pointing at it. I felt awful for you, and I wondered why she would do a thing like that to you."

"I don't remember what she said or why she did it," he says. "I've never thought that much about people's motives."

"But you must have had some feeling about what was happening ..."

"I was embarrassed."

"Embarrassed you got caught?"

"Yeah."

"Embarrassed that you were caught in my panties, or embarrassed about the erection?"

"I had no idea what an erection was."

"But when you put my panties on, this thing happened to you. Did the feel of the fabric sexually arouse you, or was it the attention you got when you got caught? Did you like how the fabric felt ... or what ... ?"

"It was the feel that made me put them on the second time, after you got into bed. And later on, the first time I ever had an orgasm, I was wearing panties, and I might have been wearing an old nightgown you had tossed out. All of a sudden ... I didn't have a clue as to what was happening, except it felt good. I didn't know what caused it at first. It happened three or four times before I figured out what was causing it, and then I learned how to make it happen myself."

This conversation eliminates any fear I may have had that Gene and I are not as close as I thought we were. This conversation is way too intimate for strangers. I am in awe of his apparent trust in me.

"When Mom took you back to bed, did you think about whether or not the embarrassment was worth the thrill? Did you think about what Mom did to you then?"

"I don't recall any thoughts so I must not have thought too much about it."

"Did I say anything to you?" I ask. "Did I tease you?"

"No. I never had any teasing from you."

I'm relieved to hear that. I don't remember everything he's telling me, so I don't remember my reactions. I'm so glad I wasn't mean.

"Did you do it again soon, or was it a long time before you wanted to do it again? Did that incident start things off?"

"I don't know if that started things," he says, "or if it was a step in that direction. I was still pretty young. A lot of things that happened during that period are a blur as far as time goes. It was probably less than a year later, when I remember wanting to put on your underwear again. Mom, Dad and you were out in the back yard working on something, and I was alone in the house. The urge to dress in girls' clothes came over me again. This time, however, instead of panties, I decided to try on a slip."

"Was it the same kind of urge, like when you decided to try on my panties?"

"Yeah, it was like that."

"How did this second adventure turn out?"

"At the age of five or so, I wasn't all that coordinated, and since I'd never worn anything like a slip, it was with considerable difficulty that I was able to get into it. But, get into it I did, and while I was admiring myself in a mirror and feeling quite girlish, I heard Mom come into the house and she began calling my name. She must have known something was up. It was her actions like that, throughout our life, that gave me this feeling that women are clued in to things that we males are not.

"As difficult as it was to get into the slip, it was impossible to get out of it, so I did the next best thing. I hid under the bed. But she found me. Busted again!

"I don't remember her reaction to what she saw, or exactly what she said, but I do remember that she was not very happy. She made me take off the slip while she was standing there, and put my own clothes back on. Twice I tried on girls' clothes, and twice I got caught. Not a very auspicious start to a new life.

"But while we were still living at that address, there was this guy named Victor, who I think had something wrong in the head. I'm not sure exactly what was wrong, and I was never directly told not to see him, but I was sort of discouraged from playing with him. I did it anyway.

"One time we were playing in the back yard and I suggested that we pretend we were girls. He was confused about that, so I didn't attempt to take it any further."

"Was that just a whim," I ask, "or did you really want to be a girl?"

"I wanted to see what it might be like to be a girl."

"Did you have any idea what you thought it would be like? Did you think I had something special going on because I was a girl? You must have gotten some ideas about what it would be like to be a girl from being with me and observing my behavior. Did you think I was a lot different from you?"

I'm full of questions. I hope I'm not pressing too hard.

"I never personalized it," he says, "or thought of it in terms of you being a girl. There's something about seeing a girl—any girl in a dress—that just appeals to me. But I believe that boys, even straight ones, have a certain attraction to girls' clothes. I know even young boys would get off on being able to see up a girl's dress, for example. I wasn't as different from other boys as you might think. When I kidded around with other boys, it was always if you got to see up a girl's dress, you got bragging rights for the day. If you got to see all the way up to her panties, then you really had bragging rights. So, there is a kind of attraction that all boys have to women's clothes … to getting to see the underwear."

I'm shaking my head. "I don't think so, Gene. Boys and men aren't looking to see underwear as much as to see what's under it, and I don't think they're thinking about what it would feel like to have the underwear on their own bodies. They want to see it on female bodies. It's the peek of the flesh that drives them, not the clothes covering it."

Gene's look tells me he doesn't necessarily agree with what I'm saying. "You told me once that you wear frilly stuff when you want to please a man," he says. "To me that means men are attracted to the same thing. There must be an attraction or you wouldn't be wearing frilly panties to please them."

"Gene, you're missing the point. The frilly panties are the tease, not the target. The clothes I put on for men are part of the personal show I put on to bring them to me. It's not the feel of the fabric on their own bodies that attracts men; it's the feel of the fabric on the woman, and more important, the feel of the woman underneath it. And that's why I wear what you call 'frilly panties.'"

"For me," he says, "seeing a woman or a girl in a cute outfit will cause me to want to dress up myself. There was this lady at work on St. Patrick's Day last spring who wore a green velvet dress. When I saw her, I could hardly wait to get home and put on my own green dress. I was literally tearing my clothes off as I was going in the door, so I could get into my dress. I wasn't attracted to her. What I wanted was to feel myself in a dress like hers. It's the feel of the clothes on me."

"Well, that's where you differ from other men."

"To me," he adds, "the most female garments are panties and a slip. I don't know if, when you were growing up, nylon had come along yet …"

"Gimme a break. I'm not that old …"

"Well, it came along after a certain point in your life. I know, because I wore a lot of your clothes, and I know the first pairs of panties of yours that I wore were not nylon.

"But still the fabric felt different from my clothes. It was a softer feel, a more sensuous feel. All the fabrics in women's clothes are softer."

I guess that answers the "who cares about fabric" question. Gene cares … a lot. So that's the deal. I think I get it. Then he continues, and it gets complicated again.

"I don't know if it's the fact of the fabric itself feeling sensuous or the fact that it's women's clothes that make the fabrics feel sensuous. If I had a man's dress shirt that had the same fabric as the blouse you have on, it wouldn't be the same."

"That sounds more like a psychological thing than a tactile thing," I say. "The same fabric in a man's style and a woman's style, and you would prefer how the woman's looks. That's not the feel, that's the look."

Gene stops talking. I think he's run out of things to say for now. I'm not quite ready to stop this discovery process. It's a new day and I want to know more. What I say next surprises me.

"Speaking of looks, I'm not crazy about the way you look in the clothes you've chosen to wear. You need some new clothes."

"I know," he says. "My clothes are getting kind of seedy. It's been hard for me to get new clothes. I used to shop by catalog and pay by check. Now they require a credit card and I don't use credit cards."

"So, get out your checkbook, Gene. We're going shopping."

"Now?" He looks scared.

"Yes. Now."

"I gotta change."

"You're right. Go change."

Today, we're not quite ready to venture out into the public arena dressed like sisters. It's way too soon for that. But someday … Who knows how we might choose to face the world?

Chapter Four

TWO GALS SHOPPING
For Mom, of course

Out the door we go to the Northgate Mall, Gene in brown cords, me in blue jeans. I chose Northgate because Gene's budget is more limited than mine and this particular mall has stores that will accommodate both of our monetary considerations. But budgets won't be the only consideration in our joint shopping venture. Gene and I have a difference in taste. A BIG difference. This mall will also accommodate that disparity.

My wardrobe leans toward a classic style, mixed with a few new fashion updates each year. Color choices are in line with my red hair, fair skin, and brown eyes—"Fall," I think they call it. So, for me it's shades of brown, green, and gold, with some red mixed in, and black, especially for evening. It's mostly solid colors, with print sometimes, in small doses; maybe a subtle glen plaid or a thin stripe, and an occasional paisley. Texture runs the gamut from silk to denim, crepe to twill.

What little I've seen of Gene's choices indicates a preference for hot pink, purple, and lime green. Black appears to be acceptable when accompanied with a lot of color relief. He obviously prefers large, bright prints, mostly floral. And from what he's told me about the feel of fabric against his skin, my guess is texture will run from silk to silkier.

Denim is not going to enter his closet. His male wardrobe has never included jeans, which is unusual for someone whose lifestyle is as casual as his. It makes sense now. Fortunately, women who are large tend to wear large patterns, so we'll probably have no trouble finding a selection of clothing to suit Gene's tastes. We'll see how easy it is for me to actually buy him something he likes. I'm definitely a fashion snob.

In the first store we visit, I notice Gene is lagging behind me a little. "Why don't we pretend we're shopping for Mom?" I offer.

I'm thinking this approach will help him relax. He nods and steps closer to me, so it looks like we're looking at choices together.

Mom's been deceased for over a decade. If her spirit has managed to survive and she's hanging over us right now, she's either terribly aghast or she's angry to see us looking at dresses for Gene, pretending we're looking for her. But this is working for us today, and at this point in our new relationship we're going to go with what works.

"What do you think about this, Gene? Do you think Mom will like this?" I ask in a tone loud enough so the clerk will know who it is we're pretending to shop for.

I don't think so, I say to myself. Mom wouldn't like this one bit. Well, that's too bad. Mom's gone and her son is here, and his wardrobe definitely needs an upgrade. Your posthumous role today, Mom, is to serve quietly as our camouflage.

My relationship with Mom wasn't a particularly close one until her last few months on earth. I knew she grew up tough and that she held herself to pretty firm standards, but as her daughter, I always wished she could have left some of that behind and relaxed and enjoyed the fruits of her struggle, and let us relax as well. It wasn't until her last year with us, when she mounted a dual crusade against the pain of her cancer and the preparation for her next life, that she was able to mellow out and let us touch a little bit of her soul. Mom's earthly exit was as magnificent and brave as her early struggles to establish a new life away from the poverty of her family's homestead.

If we seem disrespectful to the memory of her dignity by using her as a cover for our shopping for Gene's new wardrobe, let me assure you, we are not being disrespectful, or anything else close to a philosophical plane. Our thoughts and intentions aren't that deep. We're just a couple of gals enjoying a shopping spree at the mall. Sorry, Mom, if what we're doing disturbs your sleep.

Okay, now that I've put that guilt trip to rest, we forge ahead and I manage to find a couple of dresses I like for Gene, dresses that will pass his taste test as well as mine. One particular dress we both like is a modified smock in a soft wool challis, with a nice purple and olive green small floral print on a turquoise blue background. It sounds gaudy, but it's really quite acceptable. Even a fashion snob can appreciate its pattern. And I've always liked the feel of challis. I think I'll buy it for him.

HOLY COW! I just bought my brother a dress! How does that feel? You know what? It doesn't feel any different than buying a dress for anyone else. Cool. This is going to be a cinch.

While I'm thinking outerwear, because it's what I see that affirms or offends me, Gene is clearly focusing on underwear, because that's what touches his body, and that's what this cross-dressing thing seems to be about. He's finding plenty of lingerie to keep him occupied. He does enjoy sorting through those panties and slips, applying subtle little caresses as he picks them up.

"Slips are the sexiest items that women wear," he says.

"I don't wear slips. My skirts are lined."

I know, I know. From his perspective, a lined skirt is a sorry substitute for the thrill of wearing a slip. For me, a slip is an extra layer that just adds bulk. We probably had more points of agreement as brother and sister than we're going to have as sister and sister. But the former points of agreement weren't as personal as the ones to come. That's the part, I think, that may contribute to making this transition difficult at times. I'm not used to being this personal with my brother.

I'm sure we're over-explaining ourselves at the checkout stand, mumbling a bunch of unnecessary nonsense about how much our Mom needs all this underwear. The clerk's look tells me she isn't buying any of this phantom mother blather, but it doesn't matter. The cover story is for our comfort, not hers.

Loaded down with bulging shopping bags, we head to the car. We've made quite a haul. Gene's lingerie drawer will be well-stocked with new pretties. He also has a couple of decent-looking dresses that pass my criteria for soft chic, whatever that is. I just made that up. But now I can relax a bit, knowing I won't be playing sister to a floozy.

As we settle into my car, Gene is close to tears.

"I have a hard time expressing my feelings," he says, "because I've kept them under wraps for so long. I've been dreaming about a day like this my whole life. I never thought it would happen. I don't know how to thank you for this day."

His words strike me to the core. My heart literally hurts. My brother has just expressed deep, personal feelings out loud. Not his usual clever, caustic comments. I am so touched by these few words of real emotion I don't know what to say.

But there's another feeling that's creeping into my consciousness, and it's almost as strong as the acute poignancy. It's sneaking into my head, trying to overrule the tenderness that's so new to my heart.

I'm angry.

I'm angry that my brother has had to dream for so long of something as simple as a shopping day with a female companion. This is something I do without thinking at least two Saturdays a month. Having to swallow fifty years of silent yearning for something as nonthreatening as shopping for a dress to wear is so ridiculous, I can't even express the extent of my anger about it.

Society wastes so much time worrying about trivialities like who wears what and why. What the hell is this world all about anyway that we should be so uptight about such a happy, harmless activity as shopping for something attractive to put on one's own body?

But my anger is not entirely directed toward the world. Gene and I should have had years of days like this. We could have done this together in spite of public decree. We're not exactly social milquetoasts. Regardless of what Mom said or directed him to do, Gene could have told me about himself and his dreams long before this day. I'm angry at him, too. I don't know why he didn't tell me.

Oh yes, I do. And I'm not allowing myself to get away with that lame defense. It's easy to blame my mom. Aren't mothers to blame for all of life's frustrations? And it's easy to blame the one who is the subject of all this secrecy.

The truth is, Gene's apparent interest in women's clothing has been evident for quite some time. There were clues I could have seen had I been inclined to look. There were questions I could have asked, had I chosen to ask them. My justification for not asking is that I don't know how to ask personal questions. Being a tight-ass myself, I used the excuse that I didn't want to intrude on his privacy. How many times did I excuse myself on that point?

The more important question is, at what point did my excuses make me a silent accomplice to the family secret, enabling it to continue?

And still more important, deep inside, is the ultimate question: Do I actually have the same silly prejudices as the people I profess to disdain?

Nope. Not going there. Not today anyway. Probing into our deeper selves can wait. I just bought my brother a dress!

WOO HOO!!!

Chapter Five

JULIUS LA ROSA
Explanations and theories

"Gene, what is it about women's clothing that appeals to you so much? Why do you want to wear women's clothes rather than men's clothes? Is there a bottom line?"

"I've thought about that," he says. "And I don't know exactly how to answer it, except to tell you how it feels. I don't know if you remember back in the early fifties, when you had a crush on the singer Julius La Rosa. If Mom and Dad had come to you late in the afternoon and said, 'Get ready. Julius is coming by and he's going to take you out on a date,' maybe a movie or something, you know how you would have felt about that. And if they had told me that while you were gone, I could dress up in your clothes, the feeling for me probably would have been the same as for you. The same sort of rush.

"As to why women's clothes, I don't know. Humans, whether we like to admit it or not, are biological creatures and we're subject to similar mating rites as other animals. Like the way a woman looks and acts to attract a man. For some reason, that's what attracts me, but not in the sense that it attracts me to her. In my case, I want to look like her and feel what I imagine she feels, not the way he feels reacting to her. I want to feel like the girl, not the man. I guess, I kind of agree with what you said last week."

"Do you think the excitement comes from having been in the closet for so many years? Does that contribute to it?"

"I don't know that there is a way of knowing that," he says. "I think the fact that it is sort of taboo adds an element of danger, and that part probably heightens the experience. But it's not the whole experience. When I put on a dress, I feel a rush that I don't get with anything else I do."

"I guess, I'm wondering if you had been able to put on a dress all those years, when you felt like putting on a dress, would it be such a rush to put one on now?"

"Probably not as much a one," he admits. "Another thing, when you talk about cross-dressers, you're talking about men in women's clothes.

"Society's always had a totally opposite view of women dressing up. A girl, for example, who wants to wear jeans and a sweatshirt and do boy-type things, she's called a tomboy and that's okay. In fact, little girls tend to relate more to their fathers than to their mothers. Fathers are probably relieved that they don't have to deal with feminine frilly things with their daughters for a few years. It's sort of postponed. And when the time comes, the mothers step in. I'm sure that fathers are relieved when that happens. They don't have to deal with their daughters becoming women."

That seems like a pretty bizarre observation. But it kind of makes sense, though. I wonder if it's true.

"Four or five years ago" he says, "a local school district in the Seattle area proposed that they would institute a new dress code: skirts or dresses for girls, and slacks, but not jeans, for boys. The students reacted with a "dress-in" protest by showing up at school wearing outrageous clothing, including several boys who wore dresses. They even managed to get their pictures, in color, on the front page of the local newspaper.

"In my days as a schoolboy, this would have been absolutely unthinkable. For a boy to even think about dressing as a girl was considered a perversion, and to act upon those desires would make such a boy a social pariah.

"For girls, however, it was different. It was quite common for girls to wear jeans and a T-shirt, and engage in rough-and-tumble activities usually associated with boys. Many of these girls would have to be practically dragged, kicking and screaming, into wearing a dress and acting like a prim and proper young lady.

"My sister—you—could wear jeans and a T-shirt and play sports, but there was no way I could wear a skirt and blouse, and play with dolls. It simply wasn't allowed. I didn't dare mention that I even wanted to wear a skirt and blouse, much less actually wear them.

"Later, when I was managing the menswear department at Sears, two-thirds of the men's underwear were bought by women. It was wives buying for husbands. In fact, they were showing a bunch of old commercials on TV last week, and there was this one commercial where a woman was holding up a package of men's underwear, telling her girlfriend, 'now this is what you look for when you're buying this kind of clothes.'

"There's no way you'll ever see a man holding up a package of panties telling other men, 'when you're buying panties for your wife, this is what you look for.' Society just wouldn't allow that.

"And you know, every two years or so, men's boxer shorts become a women's fashion item. And I recently saw a man's dress shirt commercial where it's the wife at home, a real sexy wife. She's at home wearing her husband's dress shirt, and it's supposed to turn her husband on. You'd never see it the other way around."

Gene continues to make good points—things I've never even thought about. He goes on.

"I remember once at Sears, a husband and wife came in supposedly to buy a coat for his mother. It could have been a case like you and me shopping together, I don't know. But anyway, the deal was that he was about the same size as his mother and he should try it on, and if it fit him, it would fit her. And he did try it on, and for weeks all the store talked about was whether or not he was trying on a woman's coat for his mother or for himself. And everybody thought that was funny. That was in the women's coat department.

"But in my department, the men's clothing department, on top of the jeans rack there was a size conversion chart that showed women that if you wore a size 10 in jeans, then you wore such and such a waist in men's clothes. And that was all right. No one thought that was funny.

"So, first of all, there isn't a stigma attached to women wearing men's clothes, so there's no danger in that. But who knows if they are cross-dressers? When you see women in men's jeans, you don't know if they're cross-dressing or if they just like jeans. It doesn't seem to matter. No one asks about it, because it's accepted that women wear men's jeans.

"Maybe if a boy were borderline, and he was allowed to put on a dress, that might make him more likely to become a cross-dresser. And maybe the same thing wouldn't happen to a girl. Maybe girls aren't cross-dressers because they don't have any special feelings when they try on men's clothes."

"Something I've thought about since you came out to me is that it's a lot more difficult for cross-dressers than for gays to mingle in society. I mean, if a gay man doesn't want anyone to know, no one has to know. It's not so much about physical appearance. But when you're who you want to be, when you wear a dress, there's no hiding the fact that you're different. It makes people feel like they're forced to deal with you, and they don't like that."

"I've thought about that too," says Gene. "One day last summer we were going to the ball game together and you were late, so I looked around. There were three guys sitting behind me having a good time. I don't think they were gay, but they could have been, and nobody would have known. But if I was sitting there in a dress, everybody would know. Gays can engage in a lot of regular public behavior with their partner and no one knows the difference."

Gene looks down and pauses for several seconds, then quietly says, "But that's not possible for me."

"Throughout history there were occasions when men clearly wore women's clothing in situations where women were suppressed," I offer. "Like on the stage. Men played women's parts, and that was okay."

"Yeah, in certain professions it's okay. It wouldn't work for truck drivers."

I chuckle at that. "What do you think about the TV commercial where you see a couple of burly guys putting on makeup in a truck? When I first saw it, I thought 'Whoa!' But then it turned out to be okay, because they were just making themselves up as clowns to go to a party. First you think they're doing something they shouldn't be doing, like wearing makeup, then you figure it's okay for them to wear makeup if they're clowns. Do you have any feelings about that?"

"That wasn't so bad," he says. "But there was another one where you saw the back of someone, from the waist down, standing in a doorway talking to the woman of the house. You saw a skirt and a real girlish voice asking, 'You want to buy cookies?' And the lady says, 'Okay.' Then the camera pans back and you see this boy is walking away, pulling off his wig, and he says, 'Works every time.' That one did affect me."

"I did see it," I say, "but I didn't get it. What's the point?"

"Well, it infers that people will buy something like cookies from a little girl that they won't buy from a little boy.

"Every now and then they try to do a movie or a show on TV about cross-dressing, and I have to laugh. They have to come up with some kind of lame excuse for it to happen. Like Tom Hanks, in one of his first movies, there was a scene where two guys couldn't find an apartment. No one would rent to them so they dressed up like girls and got one. None of the guys in situations like that ever look good enough to pass for girls. It's obvious they're men. It's like only stupid people who can't see beyond their noses will accept men dressed up as women.

"There was another show on TV that was called *Ask Harry* about a real ass-hole sportswriter who was fired by his woman boss. To get even with her, he decides to start an advice column under a woman's name. He submits it under the column name, 'Ask Harriet.' It's accepted, and it's a success. That guy looked good enough to pass. There have been a few over the years that could have passed, but most of them are caricatures. It's like a sideshow freak thing."

"Does it piss you off that it seems like you have to be a woman to have the sensitivity to do something like write a column like that?" I ask.

"Nah," he says, "other than it seems to me that women do come with a gift, even as girls. When I watch you operate, it seems like you're clued into something that we're not. I don't know what that is, and I don't know why I feel that way. It's just that when women are interacting among themselves, there's something there that's unspoken, like you understand that the world operates a certain way, and we don't. I don't know how to put that into words."

"What is it you think we know something about?"

"I don't know. If I did know, you wouldn't be on that plane by yourselves."

"Like an intuition thing?"

"Yeah."

"I don't think of intuition as a group condition," I offer. "And I'm not so sure it's inherent. I think it's based on experience, and from that, expectations. But the experience has to be honest. I can pretty well predict how each of my daughters will react to certain words or situations, based on my years of experience with them. On the other hand, my relationship with you has not been honest, so now I don't know what to expect.

"Let's get back to my crush on Julius La Rosa. I'd completely forgotten about it. That would have been when I was thirteen or fourteen. Obviously, it made an impression on you. What were some things, besides my clothing, that you observed and wanted? At Christmastime, for instance, would you have asked for a doll instead of a train?"

"It wouldn't have occurred to me to dare ask for a girls' thing. But girls always get new clothes for Christmas, and when you open the packages you run into another room and try them on and come out and show them off. I always wanted to be able to do that.

"There's a thing I used to do. When the catalogs came and stayed around awhile and got old, I would take the girls' and womens' sections and cut them out minus the head and take the boys' heads and put them on and glue them into a scrapbook. Then I could see boys wearing dresses. That was cool. But it was even better when I was high school- age and I started making paper dolls.

"I'd get a stiff paper for the dolls and regular paper for the clothes. I'd get light tissue paper for see-through clothes, and colored pencils and stuff. I was doing that all through high school. Kind of embarrassing to be a high school boy playing with paper dolls, but it was fun for me. I made the paper dolls as men. A boy is still girlish enough in his features so when you put a boy in a woman's dress he might look like a girl. But with a man, you can see the contrast. You can see that it's really a man in women's clothes. And that's the rush."

"It's great that you found a creative way for you to relate," I say. "You could actually see men in women's clothes. It was the only way you could relate to other men who may have had similar feelings as you. I think that's sad. Do you try to imagine how other men like you might think?"

"I get to see it sometimes in the TV shows," he says, "but that's fakey. I saw it in the video you gave me "All Dressed Up and No Place to Go". It was interesting, but those guys were flamboyant, and I'm not that kind of person. I'm not interested in showing off and strutting. I'm not a peacock."

"Yes, and the men you see who do show off seem to have the monetary means to be more overt, more 'out there,' if you will. You can do a lot more things when you have money."

"You can pull it off," Gene adds, "if you don't have to have a real job, or if you have a job like a hairdresser, where people expect it."

"Gene, why do you think it's okay for women to wear men's clothes but it's not okay for men to wear women's?"

"For the obvious reasons. It's okay for women to do silly, crazy things, because that's all they are. They're just women ..."

I interrupt. "EXCUSE ME?!?"

"It's not me saying that," he quickly responds. "It's society saying that. Women are frivolous. They don't matter. They don't have deep thoughts. Why do you think it took a constitutional amendment to allow women to vote? Fortunately, in sports and things like that, times are changing. Nowadays, it's becoming obvious that most women can do anything they want, because they've made up their minds to do it.

"Like this whole sexual freedom thing for women. Monica Lewinsky, Bill Clinton's gal pal,was a college grad, and a smart woman. She went after the president of the United States, and if the president thought she was attractive and wanted to screw her, so what? Monica was not a victim."

"The perception, I think, is that a man is supposed to dominate," I add. "If you're a man, you've got it all, and if you're a man and acting like a woman, being submissive or responding rather than taking charge, you take yourself down a notch or two. You're demeaning the virility of manhood."

"I thought of an answer to the real men don't eat quiche thing," Gene says. "Real men can eat anything they want … including quiche. And, so can women."

"Do you remember hearing about Christine Jorgenson, who was the first person we heard about who had a sex change? I remember reading whatever I could about that."

"Have you ever had any thoughts about going in that direction?" I ask. "… going all the way to become a woman?"

"I don't think it would be as satisfying. Feeling women's clothing on my genitals is a feeling I like. It wouldn't be there if they weren't there. Does that make sense?"

"Yeah, I understand what you're saying. Basically, it's the sexual titillation you get. Do you get the same feelings from having sex—I mean sex itself, not the clothes reaction?"

"Yeah, but not with every woman. There are some women I'd like to have sex with and some women I'd rather wear their clothes than have sex with them."

I'm getting more and more curious about my sibling's feelings and attitudes toward women.

"What kinds of women do you like, Gene?"

"Oh, I don't know. The main connection has to be a brain. We had a cashier back when Farrah Fawcett was popular, and this cashier made herself up to look like Farrah and she was really gorgeous. But the only thought that ever entered her brain was about makeup and how she looked. And after about five minutes with her, the only thought I could sustain in my brain was how to stay awake. She never appealed to me, but she wore a lot of great clothes I wouldn't mind having.

"I've always liked long hair. I prefer long hair to short hair. And as far as looks, I like Asian. I like a fragile look, what I think Asian women have. And personality-wise, I like vulnerability, but not helplessness. There are times when I want to protect. I wouldn't want a woman who was totally okay on her own, who didn't need me at all."

"I guess that's why I don't have a man," I admit. "I give off this air that I can take care of myself. Well, it's not an air, actually. It's the truth. But what am I supposed to do? Fail? Would I be more attractive to the male psyche, if I were a welfare mom?"

I don't really expect an answer to that. It does kind of bother me that my brother is so much like other men with his macho attitude. I like a fragile look; I like vulnerability; I wouldn't want a woman who is totally on her own. Shit.

"So, Gene, here's a question. Are you sexually attracted to women?"

"Yeah," he says without hesitation. "There have always been girls that I have had crushes on, even when I was a boy. I don't know if other boys felt that way when they were really young, or if it was just me liking all things girly. I heard someone once describe men cross-dressers as male lesbians. You sort of want to be like a woman, but you still like women."

"That first day, when you 'outed' yourself to me, you wanted to make sure I knew that you are not gay. I didn't get the feeling that you were gay bashing, but you really wanted to establish that there is a difference between what you are and what a homosexual person is."

"Yeah. And there's a difference between me and someone like Christine Jorgensen, who was trapped in a man's body. They want men, not because they're gay, but because they're really women.

"Do you remember Renée Richards, the tennis player? She wrote a book called *Second Serve*. I used to have it, but I can't find it now. She had some homo-sexual encounters, but she was also married for a while and she sired a kid while she was a man, before her change. Reading her account when she was a boy, there was a whole lot in there I could identify with."

"Why haven't you married and had kids?" I ask. "You were so good with my kids, and now my grandkids."

"I just have too much baggage."

"Do you wish you had kids?

"Uh … (long pause) … yeah."

"In that video I gave you, there were a lot of married men, and their wives were supportive and, I'm going to make a terrible remark … the women that were married to those men didn't seem to be very bright, or have a whole lot of personal self-esteem."

"That's right," he says."But some of the men didn't either. It would be great if I could find a woman who would put up with this stuff, but I'm afraid to risk it."

"If we could eliminate the fear, and if I told you that a beautiful Asian woman called and said she was coming over to see you and she wanted to go on a date with you, possibly to dinner and a movie, would you get the same rush I would have had with a call from Julius La Rosa?"

"Yeah. If we could eliminate the fear. And if we could go back about forty years. That's two big ifs. Too big to even think about it."

A POEM

I wear panties, yes I do
In lilac, pink, and black, and blue.
Silky smooth, and lace-trimmed, too,
I love my panties, yes I do!
Over my panties I wear slips,
Cascading down around my hips.
It brings a smile unto my lips,
It's so exciting, wearing slips!
Wearing dresses can't be beat.
They make me look and feel complete.
So feminine and oh so sweet,
Wearing them is such a treat!
That is how my story goes,
To some it's troubling, I suppose.
I hope my little poem shows
How I love wearing women's clothes!

Gene Wilson

Chapter Six

MARILYN MONROE
The Sexy Ideal

Coming out after fifty years of hiding one's sexuality has to carry a certain euphoria I can't even begin to imagine. And where else can this particular euphoria be expressed except with me, in my home? It's not like the world is all of a sudden going to welcome my brother Gene in a dress. And it's not like Gene can all of a sudden throw away fifty years of being "scared shitless," as he put it, about sharing his feminine instincts.

As the weeks go by, my home becomes a veritable fashion explosion for the plus-sized woman. Let's just say the "Encore" department at Nordstrom has nothing on my very own Western Avenue Boutique.

Gene brings suitcases full of new clothes with him every weekend he's here, and he comes nearly every weekend—football game or not. He's found a few stores that have made him feel welcome to shop on his own, and the sheer numbers of his new outfits tell me his budget allows for far more fashion than I had originally assumed. He's even opened a few charge accounts. The call of the mall has brought my brother around to claiming the ultimate necessity of the 21st century, shop-til-you-drop modern woman. No woman with any kind of fashion awareness can possibly survive without a few charge cards. This is definitely a new lure for my new brother/sister.

Along with suitcases full of new clothes, Gene also brings his new camera. He has always refused to be photographed, even for the obligatory posed family holiday pictures in front of the tree. Just when we think we've successfully sneaked up on him to get a candid shot—there has to be some record of his existence among the family archives—we end up with a less than four-finger salute. Those one-finger waves are as much a part of our family albums as the fake smiles in the group photos taken without him.

I'm not sure how the pictures with Gene will be explained to future generations when they turn the pages of our 20th-century family albums and see the ill-mannered salute. But a new day has arrived, and now that he has his new "real" clothes, Gene wants me to take pictures of him in each and every new outfit, each and every weekend. I'm thinking these new pictures of Gene in the family archives will require even more adroit explanations than the middle-finger messages.

Gene knows exactly how he wants to appear in each picture. He poses in a manner that dates back to the 1950s, with an affected style that matches the clothing he's chosen to wear. As I watch him arrange his positions, I recall the movie magazines I used to buy in my preteen life. They were full of photos put out by the studios to show their stars and starlets in languid poses, wearing gorgeous gowns in lush surroundings with flattering backlights. Gene is proving to be a good student of the 1950s-style studio photo shoots.

Sometimes he stands with his feet carefully positioned in a sort of ballet Position Two—heels together, toes pointed out in opposite directions. He crosses his arms in front of him with one arm bent just enough to hold the straps of the purse that matches his shoes. Sometimes he seats himself with his feet carefully tucked back to one side or crossed at the ankles, with one arm draped across the back of the sofa.

As a teenager in the 50s, he formed his visions of what the ideal female fashion statement should look like, and that vision is unchanged. His style remains with the look of that decade; the look he has wanted to achieve all his life but couldn't, until now.

As a normal person—and I use the term "normal" facetiously—my fashion statements were allowed to evolve over the years because I got to wear each style along the way. I've gone from long pleated skirts to short leather minis, and back again. My skirts, when I wear skirts, have risen from two inches above the ankles to four inches above the knees. They come in taffeta, crepe, wool, poly cotton, silk, denim and everything in between. I've worn pants with legs of multiple lengths and dimensions; sometimes they button at the waist and sometimes they hang on the hips.

Pants also come in many fabrics, and I get to wear whatever fabric I prefer whenever they're in style, and even when they're not, if I so choose. I didn't get stuck in any singular decade of fashion, because I've been able to wear the styles of all my decades, and because I've lived my life as the socially defined "normal" fashionable female person.

But I have to confess that, even though my clothing choices have changed, when I want to look good in pictures taken for posterity, I always position my feet carefully in Position Two and make sure my hands are also carefully placed in graceful positions, not at all unlike the way my brother poses.

As I participate in Gene's nearly twenty-four-hour obsession of sharing and showing off his fashion ideas with another woman, I realize what a privilege it is for me to be able to express myself freely through fashion.

Vanity is such an important part of who we are. Being able to look into a mirror at home, or to catch a glimpse of ourselves as we pass a window along a public street and see a reflection of ourselves as we imagine ourselves to be, is a small but vital verification of who we think we are. Enduring a lifetime of seeing myself as someone I am not would be unfathomably frustrating. And I do not want to see pictures of myself as another person. Trying to understand the depth of Gene's stifled vanity helps me put a perspective on his clothing obsession.

"Marilyn Monroe has always represented the ultimate female look to me," he says. "When I see pictures and movies of her, I want to feel like she looks. I try to imagine how it must feel to have that jiggle when she walks, and how it must feel when her clothes swing and wrap around her legs."

In identifying with the Marilyn Monroe look of the 1950s, Gene was very much like that of the general population at the time. Monroe's appearance was the epitome of the 50s star look. The way she looked gave Gene a view of what represented a woman's fashion fantasy at the time he was emerging from boyhood to manhood, or whatever it was he was emerging from and going to. He was a teenager, which is the age when adult branding begins to occur for real. Marilyn was the female sexual brand that men wanted to conquer and women secretly aspired to achieve.

What Gene failed to pick up, however, was that men married June Allyson, not Marilyn Monroe. Women of that era were reared to opt for the security of marriage, rather than go for the precarious life of a sexpot. Marilyn may have represented everyone's secret desires, but men chose to settle for the girl-next-door, and women chose marriage over desire.

They also chose not to appear in daylight wearing brassy pink satin dresses with cute little bows holding their two most obvious assets in place right at the top of almost indecent exposure. Trust me. There wasn't a lot of cleavage showing on the streets of Seattle in 1956. Women may have liked the look, but they weren't wearing it.

"Do you remember that white pleated halter dress she wore in *The Seven Year Itch*?" he asks. "The one where she stood over a subway vent in New York City with air from below the street blowing the skirt up and around her waist, revealing her panties? I loved that scene, and I fantasized a lot about how wonderful it would feel. Do you remember it?"

"Of course I do," I reply. "That's the dress that drove her husband, Joe DiMaggio, over the edge with a spate of jealousy that led to their divorce."

"Yeah, well I tried that scene once," he says.

"You did wha...?"

"I found a dress that kind of looked like that dress in the old clothes throw-away bin in the basement of the house we lived in near the airport, and I made a dumb decision. It was Saturday, and I was supposed to be cleaning my room, so I had the vacuum cleaner out. It was that old bullet-shaped cleaner with the hose that could either suck stuff into the bag or blow air out the back of it, depending on where you put the hose. I'd seen the movie and I decided I could recreate that scene, using the vacuum cleaner."

"No ... You didn't!" I'm trying to stifle a giggle as my mind pictures what Gene's experiment must have looked like.

"So, there I was, on cloud nine with a blast of air blowing up my skirt against my panties, when in walked Dad."

"Oh ... my ... Gawd! What was your reaction when you saw him?"

"Oops ... I'm fucked."

No longer able to stifle the giggle, I erupt into gales of laughter. "What did he do?" I finally ask.

"He went ballistic, and before I knew what was happening, I was spread-eagled across his knee with the back of my skirt raised, receiving the worst spanking of my life. It was a bad news/good news situation. The bad news was, it hurt like hell. The good news was, with my skirt lifted up, he was spanking me directly on my panties, which felt heavenly.

"With each blow he would yell over and over ... 'Do you want to be a girl? ... Do you want to be a girl?' I, of course, lied each time and said no."

That had to have been a horrible moment for Gene. I compose myself as best I can, in an attempt at empathy. "Did he make you take off the dress?"

"He just told me to get out of it ... and he left."

"Do you think that was the first time for him to see you in a dress when you were more grown up?"

"As far as I knew, it was the first time since my two ill-fated attempts at ages four and five, and he didn't even see me when I was five. I had managed to avoid getting caught for several years, for a couple of reasons. One was that I had gotten a little smarter with age. But mainly, it was because we had moved to the house south of Seattle, where you and I had our bedrooms in the basement, and he and Mom mostly stayed upstairs on the main floor. That greatly improved my secretive situation."

"What was your reaction? I mean, how did you feel when he was beating on you? Were you scared?"

"No. I felt I had it coming."

"Oh God. How awful! How old were you when it happened?"

"I don't know … twelve or so, I guess. I didn't blame him. I tried to imagine how he felt, seeing his only son standing in a dress with a vacuum cleaner hose blowing air up his ass."

He grins. That's all the cue I need to start laughing again. What my mind is seeing is too much to overcome. Okay, okay. Settle down, girl.

"Did he just go away?" I ask. "Did he ever mention it again?"

"Not with me."

He says that quietly, and with a sense of finality.

"Did your relationship with Dad change after that, or was there ever a relationship to begin with?"

"We were never buddy, buddy close. But we were about as close as I ever was with anybody. You see the TV shows and movies about guys and their dads bonding and all that, and when the dad gets old and the son's in his middle years, they have this great relationship. I never felt anything like that."

"Of course, Dad died when you were twenty years old," I remind him, "so that couldn't happen. What do you think of him now?"

"I didn't know him that well," he says. "He was a great guy and all that, sensitive and fun and stuff. But as far as me knowing him personally, I didn't really know him. He and I were people who didn't need to say a lot, so maybe there was more there than I thought."

The three of us, Dad, Gene, and I spent a lot of time together, especially on weekends when Mom was at work. We went to minor league baseball games almost every weekend to watch Seattle's Triple A team, the Seattle Rainiers. We went fishing together; we combed bookstores together looking for stories about the settling of The Old West. That was Dad's favorite literary subject.

Later, when we grew up, Dad and Gene drove me to college in Colorado and they continued on to visit major league ballparks in the Midwest. The thrill of seeing Stan Musial playing in St. Louis, in a major league stadium, is an experience Gene still talks about.

Even more significant, I think, is that they also went to Arkansas to see where Dad was born and raised. On Dad's first trip back to his boyhood hometown, he elected to take his son with him. I've never seen Black Oak, Arkansas, with or without Dad.

I wonder how much all of that counted with Gene, or if he was so preoccupied with where he was going to get his next dress fix, that such experiences went unnoticed and underappreciated. I think Gene probably shared more with his Dad than he remembers. It's too bad Dad died so young. If he'd lived longer, perhaps they would have shared more, and their relationship would be better-remembered.

These are useless thoughts. Dad is gone and there are other issues that need to be addressed. For one, Gene accepts ridicule and humiliation much too readily. His "I felt I had it coming" attitude truly disturbs me. We have to find a way to get him past this feeling of shame when he talks about his feminine side. It is so contrary to the intellectual, smart-ass posture he carries when he's wearing pants.

But right now, my moment of ennui is overcome by my imagining the Marilyn Monroe scene again—the bullet-shaped vacuum cleaner with its hose in the "other" end, the pleated dress blowing up in the air ... and the smile of contentment he must have had on his face right before he got caught. I'm laughing again. I can't help it. Poor Gene, poor Dad. But how about poor me? I can't stop laughing ... my sides are killin' me!

Gene waits for me to settle down. Okay. I'll try. There. I just about have it under control.

Then thoughts of Marilyn bring me to thoughts of her husband, the Baseball Hall of Famer Joe DiMaggio, and I lose it again. Our very own dad, a transformed Arkansas hobo, and Joltin' Joe DiMaggio, a national hero, had something in common. The Hobo from Arkansas and the Yankee Clipper, both now deceased, are joined together by a common disgust directed at a beautiful white, pleated halter dress worn by Gene's secret idol, Marilyn Monroe, a half-century ago. It was my brother, the cross-dresser, who formed the connection that brought these manly men together in an undisclosed common cause. Six degrees of separation? I'm laughing again. Can't help it.

Gene continues to look at me with more than a little forbearance as he waits for me to get myself under control, so he can continue with a conversation he obviously wants to complete.

"For some reason," he says, "just watching how the skirt sort of moves around her legs, attracts me to her … to Marilyn. I want to look like that, and feel like that. I want to feel like a girl. Women have a certain look, and I have an idea in my head of what it's supposed to feel like when they wear silky fabrics and walk a certain way.

"There was one time when I'd been out driving at night in Bellingham and I had on women's clothes. I don't know if it was just the right combination of panties, slip and dress, and maybe the right shoes, but walking from my car to my back door, I got this feeling. It felt like what it looked like to me, when I watch a beautiful woman walk. I felt like I'd discovered the feeling and I didn't want to stop walking. I wanted to keep going, just because it happened to feel right, and I didn't know if I'd ever get that feeling again."

"And did you?" I ask.

"There was another time, when I first started going out at night for walks. I don't know. It was the right combination of hosiery and skirt … it just felt right …"

"Night walks? Wearing a dress?" I ask. I'm getting a creepy feeling.

"Yeah, we'll talk about that some time."

The thought of my brother taking late-night walks in a dress immediately settles me down … for good. This is not funny. He's scaring me.

Chapter Seven

THE CLOTHES BIN
Gene's secret stash

"Were there any other incidents that you remember—moments that stand out?"

"Well, there was another time when we lived on 48th Avenue. The Johnson family lived across the street. Mrs. Johnson took care of us when Mom went to work. One of her daughters, Carol, had a paperback book that had pictures with drawings of people from around the world. One page had a picture of Scotland with a boy in a kilt, and to me that was like seeing a boy in girls' clothes, and every chance I got I'd sneak a look at that. Actually, I remember now that I tore out that page and took it home."

"I remember an incident with Carol at their house," I recall. "I think she had inclinations toward wanting to be a boy. They had a coal furnace and Carol decided one day she wanted to pee like a boy, and she opted to do it in the coal bin. Her mom caught her—what is it with mothers and their sleuthing?—and she beat the crap out of her. She used a willow switch. Parents seem to feel they have a right to strike their kids when they do something that makes them mad or confused."

"I don't remember that," Gene says, "but I always thought she would grow up to be … I don't know, I always thought she would make a better-looking boy than a girl.

"Another thing while we were on 48th Avenue. One year at Jefferson grade school—it would have been the first or second grade—I remember a boy on Halloween came in wearing a dress, a Little Orphan Annie-type dress. He had a bandana sort of thing tied around his head, and I thought that was pretty cool. I took special notice, but to everybody else it was probably just a Halloween costume.

"And there was another time, which may or may not have actually happened. I just seem to recall it. I think Mom sent me to school wearing panties to punish me for not getting my clothes into the laundry room in time for the wash."

"Yes, I recall something like that."

"I remember we were walking along Erskine Way to school, and I was feeling pretty smug about my so-called punishment …" His look turns smug right now.

"Yes, I do remember it," I say, "and in retrospect it seems curious she'd do that, given your history at the time. Curious as hell. I wonder if Mom did it on purpose to make panties a form of punishment so you wouldn't want to wear them so much."

He ignores my comment. "That's as much as I can remember from 48th Avenue. It was when we moved south of town that I started dressing up more. It probably had to do with a bunch of things, like being older and more aware of wanting to do it, especially since it was having a more sexual effect. And probably it had to do with having more privacy. We had our own bedrooms by then.

"And later on, I don't know if you remember, between the laundry area and the shower downstairs there was a kind of a cabinet thing. That's where I got the Marilyn Monroe dress. A lot of old clothes got thrown in there that we weren't wearing anymore. There were always some panties and some skirts, and I could take them to my own room. And by having this stash of clothes that nobody was wearing, if I did borrow something of yours, you were not likely to miss it right away.

"If I borrowed something from your bedroom, that might be the next thing you wanted to wear. Sometimes I went into your room, but I would always be running the risk of being caught in your room, either getting your clothes or trying to put them back. It helped reduce the risk by having these other clothes that were easier to get."

"Did the easy access reduce the thrill?"

"I don't know. There was still the risk of being caught."

"Okay, sometimes you went to the old clothes bin and sometimes you borrowed clothes from my room. Did you ever feel you were invading my privacy by going into my closet or chest of drawers? Did that occur to you?"

"Later on, it did—after the fact."

"You just had to do it? Did you feel guilty about it?"

"Yeah."

"What made you feel guilty, invading my privacy or wearing my clothes?"

"Wearing your clothes."

"Was the guilt that you were not supposed to wear women's clothes, or that you were wearing my clothes?"

"I wasn't supposed to be wearing any women's clothes ... including yours."

He doesn't understand what I'm trying to get to; he was invading my privacy and betraying a trust. It's not registering with him. Move on. Learn more.

"Did the article of clothing itself attract you ... were there certain items that you especially liked?"

"As far as individual items of apparel, I don't have any specific memories of any one item, probably because I was doing it so much more, there was less focus on each time."

"How much more?"

"Like if I was at home sick, I would dress up while you were at school. One summer you went away to camp, and I dressed up then. And you went to Canada one time with the Girl Scouts. At that time, I started experimenting with lipstick. A few weeks after that, Mom announced that somebody had been messing with her lipstick and that it had happened about the time you went to Canada, so she probably knew it was me."

"That would have been when I was about eleven or twelve, so you were ten or eleven. By then you were doing this dress-up thing a lot?"

"Quite a bit."

"Why?"

"Just because I could, I guess. It's like the old joke as to why a dog licks his balls. Because he can. I was dressing up more because I could. I was wearing your old panties under my own clothes almost every day."

• • • • •

"Do you remember Dale and Dennis? They were twins that lived across the street from us. You had some panties that were white with striped panels on the legs; some were blue and white, some red and white. I was wearing a pair of them one day, over at their house. We were playing baseball in front of their garage and someone hit a foul ball that went over it. We spent most of the afternoon looking for it. At one point, I was bent over and the waist of the panties was sitting above the waist of my pants and one of the boys noticed. He started laughing and pointing. 'You're wearing girls' underpants!'

"You came to my defense. 'That's not true,' you said. If that was true, it would be my underwear, and I don't have any underpants that look like that.'

"You were always defending me."

Gene's stories of our past bring some recollections to me, but my memories are different from his. Maybe they're just incomplete. I remember losing the baseball and looking for it, but I don't remember the panties part of it, which is odd. If that part was inconsequential enough for me to forget it, why did it seem important enough for me to step up and defend him? We're talking about kids who were fairly young and certainly not sexually aware. At least I wasn't. So, it seems strange that I would feel the need to defend him. Maybe it was the teasing. I don't like teasing. Never have.

"There were other times when I'd wear your panties," Gene said, "when we went on camping trips, or visits to the relatives in Oregon. I'd stash a couple pair of panties in the bottom of my sleeping bag, and I'd put them on at night while I was inside the bag. I got pretty good at doing that. I was always scared, though, that someone would find out. I don't know why I'd keep doing it, being scared as I was."

"Why do people go to horror movies?" I offer. "Some people just get off on being scared. Maybe that's your shtick. Maybe part of why you do it is the scare factor. Maybe that's why you choose to lead this double life."

"I never thought about it as leading a double life," he says. 'Dressing up' was just something I did. And I never thought of it as being something as big as a lifestyle. It would be the same thing as if I did some other annoying thing. Like ... whatever ... like cutting down a tree in the neighbor's yard. It was just something I did.

"I don't look for deeper meaning," he continues. "I learned not to worry about things I can't control. I've always been sort of that way. It was never like, 'Why am I doing this', or 'Am I being cheated', or 'Is God being cruel to me'? That kind of stuff never came up in my mind. I was always looking for new things to wear, and anything that found its way into the clothing bin became mine. That's all I thought about."

"Didn't anyone ever figure out that clothing disappeared from there?" I ask.

"Well, I think it was old clothes they weren't going to wear anymore. Maybe they were going to take them to the Goodwill some day, but because they weren't part of the regular clothes routine, they forgot about them. I do remember a white dress you had that had blue flowers on it. On the end of our garage there was a kind of shed, and I remember taking that dress out there with the idea of going back after it got dark and putting it on and wandering around outside for a while."

These are amazing disclosures to me. What I am hearing is that my brother spent his entire childhood plotting secret maneuvers to get to put on my underwear and dresses. That's what he remembers about our relationship. He doesn't remember our playing, or talking, or doing anything else together. He remembers only this overwhelming, unrelenting drive to put on my clothes. At least that's how it seems.

And there I was, lah-de-dah-ing all along, aware only of the passing of time through what I thought was a fairly uneventful childhood; thinking we were in this time of life together, just like all our friends and families. How could I have been so oblivious to what was really going on?

It boggles my mind that Gene remembers the tiniest things in such detail, like stripes on panties and blue flowers on a white dress. I've forgotten most of my dresses. They were just clothes to me, part of a lifetime of garments hanging in my closets for the sole purpose of keeping my body covered. Yes, I remember a few that I wore for special occasions, but it was the occasions that stood out. The dresses were part of the occasions, not the purpose of the occasions for these long-forgotten clothes.

Gene, on the other hand, had an emotional attachment—not to the occasions, but to my not-so-forgotten clothes. The clothes were the event. They were the reason he got up each morning. They were his life's pursuit. They were facts to me, emotions to Gene.

I had a white dress with flowers. Fact. Nothing remembered. He saw a white dress with blue flowers. It was forbidden fruit and it became part of a secret pursuit, filled with emotion. Memorable.

Perhaps if I'd had some of Gene's daily intrigue, my growing up would have been more memorable for me too. I'd have remembered that white dress ... and its blue flowers.

"Did you extend your urges to anything else female," I ask, "like playing with my dolls? Did you put dresses on my dolls, or anything like that?"

"Well, I did play with paper dolls," he says. "I made my own. I made boy paper dolls and put girls' clothes on them. But that was later on. I think that was when I was in high school. We talked about that already."

"Other than when you were little, and when Dad caught you being Marilyn Monroe, were there any other confrontations? Or did you manage to lead this secret life for the most part without interference?"

"I think Mom must have suspected all along. She's the one who caught me, early on. And then later, when I got bigger and started wearing her clothes, she probably knew for sure."

I am floored. "You wore her clothes too?!? Oh my God! Talk about risky. Was the urge that strong, that you just had to take the risk?"

"Sooner or later I'd have to risk it," he says. "On any specific day I could choose not to, but sooner or later the urge would get to be too strong to ignore. It's like sociopath Ted Bundy could say 'I'm not going to kill anybody today, but down the road ...'"

That's a chilling correlation. I'm not sure I want to follow that up. "Did you ever try to resist when the urge overtook you, or did you just go with the flow?"

"Go with the flow..."

"If you got to put on a woman's clothes for a whole afternoon or longer, did that tend to satisfy you for a longer period of time?"

"It tended to make me want it more."

"You seem so intent on experiencing how it feels to be a woman. Do you ever wish that you were a woman?"

I know I've asked myself this question before, and I'll probably ask it again. This is so puzzling to me. These are such strong emotions with no follow-through to what seems to me to be a natural progression.

"I know someone who made the physical change from man to woman," he says, "so, I know it's a possibility, but it doesn't appeal to me. The satisfaction just wouldn't be there. The thrill comes from being a man in women's clothing, not a woman in woman's clothing."

Cross-dressing, as Gene describes it, is simple. It's all about the feel of feminine clothing and feminine fabrics touching the hard, coarse male body. A person could look for a deeper point to cross-dressing. I suppose one could insinuate that it's the ultimate soft next to hard, female against male, caressing bodies expressed in clothing. But from what I can gather in my very brief period of personal knowledge, through Gene, it doesn't go that deep. Nothing about this seems to have any deep meaning. It appears to be a clothes fetish, and that's all.

To be perfectly honest, I would feel more satisfied with the time I am spending on this subject, if I could find a deeper meaning associated with it. Pursuing the contents of an old clothing bin, just because he could, seems like a pursuit of not very much. But there is that risk factor attached to it. Maybe that's it. I don't know.

I guess I just don't get it yet.

Chapter Eight

HIS MOTHER-DAUGHTER DREAM
The mother I wanted

Gene spoke to me at length about how he wished he had a mother-daughter relationship, like he imagined and observed I had with our mother. One day he spoke at length about this. I let him talk for as long as he wanted to, without interruption. Here is what he shared, in his own words.

"In life, it's normal for fathers to have special relationships with their daughters, and mothers to have the same specialness with their sons. For me, it was a little different. For a normal boy, I supposed a typical high point in his relationship with his mother would be when she drove him to his football or baseball game. She'd give him a victory hug after the game, and they'd go home to make him a plate of cookies to celebrate.

"In my case, if I were to write the script, she would take me shopping for dresses, give me a hug, and tell me how cute I looked in my new dresses, and then we'd return home where I'd slip into a casual skirt and blouse so as not to soil my new dress while she taught me how to make cookies. In short, I would have loved more than anything to have had my mother's approval and support to dress as a girl so we could do girl things together. However, as I related earlier, society had a zero-tolerance policy with regard to boys dressing as girls, and my mother was very much a part of that society. The few times she actually saw me dressed as a girl, I received nothing but complete disapproval.

"There were many times when I wished I had the courage to ask for permission to dress up, but I could never go through with it. I learned early on that any feelings of what it would be like to be my mother's daughter would have to come from my own imagination.

"My fantasies of being my mother's daughter were mostly inspired by observing the two of you interacting, and then mentally placing myself in your shoes. I didn't imagine myself replacing you as her only daughter. I saw myself as the other daughter, sharing the experiences with you.

"For example, there was one time when you were sitting next to Mom on the couch. We had just gotten the latest Sears catalog, and you were going through it, page by page, discussing the pros and cons of all the fashions. I imagined myself, not as being the one with Mom instead of you, but as wearing a dress of my own, sitting next to Mom on the other side of her and sharing my likes and dislikes with both of you.

"Another time, when the two of you were talking, the name Zina Bethune, a TV actress, came up and you, in jest, complained that you should have been given a similarly exotic name. It made me think of how often I've thought about what female name I'd like to have. For the record, my name of choice was Susan. Susan was dignified-sounding, for when I wanted to appear mature and lady-like. Suzie or Suzie-Q would then be perfect for when I was in a whimsical or girlish mode.

"In my ideal world, my mother would embrace my desire to dress like you, in a dress, and think of me as her other daughter, as my sister's little sister. In fact, her reaction was just the opposite. My mother only saw me in girls' clothes a few times throughout my life, which we've already talked about. Wearing girls' clothes resulted not in acceptance but in disapproval, embarrassment, shame, and punishment. So, even though my desire to dress as a girl was strong, the fear of being caught meant I had to be smarter and take better precautions to avoid discovery.

"When I was home alone, I could get pretty active. I walked around a lot, sometimes twirling around to see and feel my dress billowing out. When I went to the kitchen for a snack, I'd stand up on my tiptoes and reach up to the top shelf in order to feel my dress slide up and down against my legs and panties. And I loved the feeling of tucking my dress under me as I sat down.

"I also spent a lot of time in front of a mirror, where I could see myself as a girl. I liked what I saw. I'd practice posing in my most young-ladylike manner. Typically, dressing up meant wearing a slip and panties, and either a skirt and blouse, or a dress. Most of the time, I would put on your shoes. Being a year younger than you, as a boy, I was small enough to fit into your clothes and shoes. As I approached my teenage years, I grew into Mom's dress size, which made my wardrobe considerably larger.

"As I reached my preteen years, I began to experiment with makeup. I'd apply Mom's rouge, eye shadow, and lipstick. I loved wearing lipstick! It made me feel pretty, and what young girl doesn't want to feel pretty?

"One evening, while the four of us were sitting at the table for supper, Mom announced that someone had been using her lipstick. She said it happened while you were away in Canada on a Girl Scout trip. She didn't actually accuse me, but she was looking directly at me when she spoke. It was obvious that she, and you and Dad, believed it was me who got into her makeup. I hemmed and hawed and offered some sort of feeble claim of innocence, which fooled no one.

"To my surprise, Mom dropped the subject. The message she sent was that she was on to me. The message I received was that I needed to be more careful. From then on, before I borrowed a slip or panties, I would take careful note of how they were folded and located, so when I returned them, they would appear to have been untouched. I did the same thing with blouses and dresses from the closet, and with her cosmetics. It apparently worked well enough that it would be several years before she saw her other daughter again.

"Because of fear of embarrassment and shame, I went to great lengths to keep my secret life hidden, but deep down inside, I wanted to come clean. Usually, I was able to keep this on hold, but every now and then the desire to come out would rise up within me to the point that I had to struggle against the urge to shout out to anyone who would listen, 'My name is Gene, and I want to dress as a woman, and I don't care who knows it!'

"One Friday evening, the urge to come out was particularly strong. I tossed and turned all night, unable to sleep. I was still awake the next morning, when I heard Mom up and about in her bedroom next to mine. Then I heard her come out of her room, and I emerged from my room wearing a pink A-line skirt and white ruffled blouse, mumbling something about wanting to talk.

"I don't remember much about what was said. We were both good at avoiding the issue. I couldn't bring myself to talk openly about wearing women's clothes. And she was unable to deal with the fact that her son would rather be her daughter. The only thing I remember specifically was that I was not to dress up in front of you again.

"I remained dressed in my skirt and blouse for most of the weekend. I stayed mainly in my room, but I did come down for breakfast on Sunday morning. I could see how much it pained her to see me in women's clothes, so for the rest of the day I changed clothes before coming out of my room. That was the last time she ever saw me dressed up.

"The subject never came up between us again. Many years later, when she was dying with cancer, I was torn about whether or not to bring it up. On the one hand, I felt that it might be helpful to bring some sort of closure, but on the other hand, I thought it might cause unnecessary pain in the time she had left. In the end, I said nothing, but I'm still not sure that was the right thing to do."

Chapter Nine

MOM DEALS WITH THE PROBLEM
Or not

"Gene, it makes me so sad to hear what you've just said about wanting to be my sister for so long. I had no idea. Can you describe your current feelings about Mom?"

To my surprise, he gives me a kind of dismissive shrug, like who cares? Then he offers, "Most of the memories I have of her now, fortunately, are from later, as she was preparing to leave this life. As a boy growing up, I hoped to have a personal relationship with her, but like I said, she avoided it. She was afraid of where it would lead. I also felt she gave a little too much of herself to her work, and not enough to us. But she changed a lot over time, I think, as we all grew older."

"She did change and, like you said, we became closer when she got cancer," I add. "But mostly I remember her as needing a lot of personal attention. You wanted what you thought we had, but we really didn't have that much mother-daughter time either. You and I never were Number One in her life, like you might expect from a mother. She needed to be center stage."

"She had a tendency to try too hard," Gene says. "It wasn't enough when we did something cool. She had to embellish everything. It wasn't enough that I was a banjo player. She had to tell everybody that I was one of the best banjo players in the world, and sometimes she would embarrass me that way by going overboard. But I didn't resent it or anything, because I knew she wanted to do the right thing, and my situation only made it harder for her."

"I didn't have any particular parental feeling with her either, like … wow, she's my mom, and isn't she special," I respond. "Maybe it's just not that easy, this parental thing. When I held my daughter for the first time, I know I didn't feel a sudden rush of motherly emotion. I didn't know how I was supposed to feel. I had nothing, really, to draw from.

"But that's a whole other story we don't need to go into now. Fortunately, the bonding with my daughters did happen. And Mom certainly connected with them. She was crazy about her grandkids. But she and I weren't that close. To a certain extent, like you, it happened with Mom and me when she got sick. I think all of us came together those last few months. Better late than not at all, I guess.

"Gene, I know there was at least one memorable encounter you had with Mom, besides the incidents when you were little. Let's talk about that.

"It happened when you were about fifteen. We had moved back to downtown Seattle by that time. Mom and I had been shopping. When we got home, all the drapes were drawn. I didn't know why, but Mom immediately knew what was going on. She said, 'Shirleyanne, you wait here.' I sat down in the living room and she went upstairs."

"If I was dressed up, I would have closed the drapes," he said. "There were close houses on both sides of us then. There were windows and doors where we could see into each other's houses, and I'd have made sure the drapes were all closed."

"Then there must have been more incidents that you've not shared with me, leading up to this day. Why would she know something was going on, just because the drapes were closed?"

"I was wearing one of your dresses, and you'd been looking for it. I don't know if you remember the dress. It was gold, with maybe some black in it. I was wearing that with the petticoats and everything."

I know which one he's talking about, but I wasn't looking for it. It was an evening dress. This incident occurred in the middle of the day, like I said, and Mom and I were just coming home. What happened downstairs was just as I described. But I'm not going to challenge Gene, because most of what we're trying to discover in our conversations is what each of us remembers, and like I mentioned, sometimes we remember things differently.

Gene continues. "Right next to my room there was a small attic room and I was hiding in there. She came and opened the door and I was standing there. I had your shoes on, too, to complete the whole outfit."

"You heard us come in and you were in your bedroom wearing my clothes, and you ran into the attic and hid. Then you heard one of us coming up the stairs. Were you scared?"

It seems like I ask that question a lot. He must have spent at least half of his lifetime being scared.

"I guess. More like resigned. It was like when I was hiding under the bed when I was little."

"What did you think was going to happen?"

"I didn't know."

"What did happen?"

"She told me to get out of your dress, and while I was changing, she made an appointment for me with Dr. Jacobs."

"As I recall, she came downstairs and told me you were wearing my dress. Then she asked, 'Do you know if he's ever worn your clothes before?' And I said no.

"She said, 'Well something happens when he wears your clothes. You would have noticed.' And then she told me she was taking you to see Dr. Jacobs. What happened with Dr. Jacobs?"

"He took me into his office and he started—I guess fondling is the right word—to see if that was going to arouse me, and it didn't. He was probably thinking in terms of me being gay. If a man was fondling me, and if I was gay, I would have an erection. And I didn't. He kept questioning me, 'Do you like this, or do you like that' ... or whatever."

"The term cross-dressing, or transvestite, didn't come up?"

"I think Mom said something about that and he said—gay wasn't a word that was used back then—I don't know what word he used. Maybe he used the word homosexual. But he said I wasn't that and he wasn't exactly sure why I would want to be in a dress, because I didn't seem to be partial to boys."

"That was all that happened there?"

"Yeah."

"And on the way to see Dr. Jacobs, or on the way home, did Mom say anything to you?"

"She talked so much, most of the time I just tuned her out. So, she could have been talking and I probably wouldn't have heard her."

"Was there any follow-up conversation?"

"I don't remember. I think for her, and for Dad, denial was the easiest thing to do. If you ignore something, you think it's not happening."

This doesn't square with me. Mom confronted the issue enough to take Gene to a doctor, and then nothing? She was in awe of doctors. She thought they were all wise. Maybe she figured if our doctor couldn't tell her anything about Gene, then no one could, so she dropped it. Or maybe she'd finally hit a problem she couldn't solve by sheer will, and she just didn't know what to do. But she was Gene's mom, and moms don't stop trying.

"Did you and she ever discuss these things again?"

"Well, later on," he said, "after I was in the Air Force, and I went to college, we had that … encounter, I guess you'd call it, with the pink skirt, that I talked about.

"I was living at her house while I decided what was next in my life. Dad, as you know, had died before then. I did a similar deal with her like I did when I came out to you. I appeared downstairs, from my room, dressed in a skirt and blouse. It wasn't my first time with her, but it had been a long time."

"Wait a minute," I interrupt. "After the doctor day, nothing happened? You went through high school and you went away to the Air Force, and you went to the university long enough to graduate, and in all those years nothing ever came up?"

"No."

"Then one day, out of the blue, you decided you wanted her to know it was still a happening thing. Why, after all this time?"

"By then you were married and you had your own daughters, Rebecca and maybe Shannon, too. I could tell Mom was thinking of me as being perverted, and she was worried that I would do something involving them. So, she made an appointment for me to see a psychiatrist. I went one time, and he ended up doing all the talking. I couldn't open up with him. Maybe, if it had been a woman psychiatrist, or if I had worn a dress during the session, it might have worked out differently. Nothing ever came of that appointment. It was one time only."

"Because I had small children, she was worried, and still she didn't talk about it? She just made an appointment for you one day?"

"Yeah. She probably was still thinking it was something that could be cured. Then, like I said, I sat around in the kitchen until she started fixing dinner. After a while, I went upstairs and changed into my regular clothes because I could tell she was upset about it."

"Wait … wait a minute! Let's go over this again. You went downstairs in a pink skirt, et cetera, and you had lunch together, and she said what? What happened at lunch? Did you talk at all?"

"I don't remember exactly."

See, this is one thing I don't get. He can remember the smallest detail of a pair of panties he wore when he was four years old, but he can't remember what happened during an important encounter that could have determined the outcome of how he would live his life. And every time he and I meet to talk about this, I have to probe hard to draw out even the smallest pieces of information that he does remember.

It was Gene who asked me to write his story, but I can't get him to expand on anything except the color or feel of a certain dress or a pair of panties he wore on a certain day. That afternoon with Mom is important, but he doesn't recall any conversation they may have had. The color of the skirt he wore is secondary, at best. But that's me thinking from my perspective. Obviously, it's not what Gene thinks. He puts the skirt over the conversation, if there was a conversation. I hate the idea that my brother is so shallow. I simply have to probe some more.

"Did she just pretend that nothing was going on? Did she allow you to talk about what was happening?"

"We didn't talk about it," he says.

"You didn't talk about it. The two of you sat down at the table and had lunch together, and NOTHING?"

"Yeah."

"Is that what you expected when you decided to have this encounter?"

"I didn't know that I was expecting anything. You know …"

Gene pauses a long time and I decide to wait him out. Finally, he speaks.

"At least I got it off my chest. That was the main thing that I got out of it. And her reaction was enough that I could tell that she was not comfortable with it at all."

"GENE! This is making me crazy! Comfort, Hell! Mom wasn't a comfort person. She was a warrior. She loved being in the middle of solving people's personal crises. It was her favorite thing to do. Wade in and take care of everything, save the day, and all that. And then accept the accolades for doing so. But her actions with you, it was just denial. Total denial. How can that be comfortable?"

"Except," he says. "I was different from being someone else's problem. I was her son. It's not something she could deal with publicly without it reflecting on her. There was nothing she could think of to tell people. She couldn't fix it. She only talked about problems she could fix."

"Yes, and that was my primary problem with her," I grumble. "What other people thought counted for everything. Who we were and what we thought counted for nothing. I never had heart-to-heart talks with her. She wasn't interested in private conversations. All she wanted was a public forum where people could gasp and admire her.

"The fact that you got your degrees in Chinese and Japanese and went to Yale and graduated from the University of Washington, and got fabulous offers from the United States Government, and all that, she talked and talked and talked about. She was so excited about your possibilities, and you chose not to go any further. You stayed at home and put on dresses. It had to have been a major disappointment for her. So, she didn't talk about it.

"When I told her that I was getting a divorce, the first thing she said to me was, 'I don't know what I'm going to tell people.'"

"And this with me," Gene says. "Well, again, there was nothing she could tell people."

"You're right. If she couldn't tell people about something, she didn't spend her time on it."

"I don't know," he says. "At least in my case, I don't know if it was so much that she didn't care. She just didn't know how to deal with it. I can see in your case where you have resentment with her not caring because it was stuff she should have been able to deal with. It wasn't a big deal. But for a mother whose son is wearing a dress—that is a big deal. And it's a lot to throw on anybody."

Here we go again. Nothing that involves me is important. Divorce? Raising two children alone? And let me assure you, I was indeed alone on that one. He thinks that's nothing. It's not important because I'm a girl, and girls are frivolous. Mom worried about herself and her image, and Gene worried when his next wearing of my panties and dresses would occur. Like, that's not frivolous. Panties and dresses, slips and purses, blah, blah, blah . . . sure Gene, that's deep. That's about skin-deep.

Choke it down, Shirleyanne. Remember your role as the good listener. No one wants to hear your sob stories. They're too frivolous. Damn! I'm really pissed off. Gotta get a grip.

"You're accepting too much responsibility for Mom's failure to communicate and empathize," I toss out, as I attempt to put a lid on my anger.

"And you're expecting too much from her," he throws back at me. "It's just that I understand what the situation is and how people feel about it. I don't feel guilty for causing them to feel that way, but I do understand that they do feel that way."

"Denial is not parenting."

"It's a lot to ask a parent to deal with."

"It is NOT!"

Gene's chuckling now. "Is too."

"She's a parent and she didn't even try. That's inexcusable."

"I don't feel as strong about it as you do."

"Maybe I feel strong about it because I'm a parent and you're not. A parent doesn't say, 'if only.' A parent can say, 'I don't understand' or 'tell me about it.' That's not so difficult. And it's not too much to ask. But you're right, it would be asking too much of her."

"Especially in those days," he says.

"Yes, I know. Those days were different. But there had been enough incidents that when you appeared in front of her that day, you obviously needed some response from her, and she did nothing. That's worse than saying the wrong thing. That's making you invisible. That's denying you exist. That's worse than anything, period."

Gene doesn't understand how important this issue is with me. And I don't really know why it's so important, which may be why he doesn't understand it. And I just decided I don't care to get into it any further right now. I get to have my denial time, too.

Chapter Ten

SPY TIME
Under wraps in the Air Force

"We've not talked about your time in the Air Force, Gene. I was married and living in Alaska at the time, so that part of your life is kind of sketchy to me. I heard from Mom that you enlisted in the Air Force, and they sent you to Yale to study Chinese. I thought you were studying engineering or something at the University of Washington. What did I miss?"

"Yeah, I was at the U Dub then. I was enrolled in aeronautical engineering because that made sense, with my interest in planes and with Boeing being here and all. But I found I wasn't interested so much in engineering. I got bored and started screwing around and my grades started dropping, so I quit school and looked around for something else to do."

"Was that when you signed up for the Air Force?"

"At first, I looked at the Air Force Academy. I wanted to fly airplanes. Mom liked that idea and she did some work to get one of our senators to sponsor an entrance exam. It was pretty easy and I passed with high scores. But my eyes kept me out. You remember, I punctured my eye with a chisel when I was about three, and I had to wear glasses. They were looking for perfect specimens then. They were afraid if for some reason I lost my glasses, I'd destroy a plane or something."

"That must have been disappointing," I said. "So, you joined the regular Air Force and they sent you to Yale to study Chinese. How'd that happen?"

"After Basic Training, everybody took tests to get their final assignments, and they'd seen my other test scores from when I tried for the Academy. So, they put me in a special group that tested for language skills. I wanted to get into the German group so I could go to Germany and buy a Porsche when I got out, and have it shipped home. But that didn't work out. Apparently, I showed some skills they thought were better-suited to learning Chinese."

"Too bad about that, huh?" I say sarcastically. "From that disappointment you got to go to Yale, then to the Far East where you discovered you enjoyed not only their language, but also their culture. Talk about landing on your feet after your original plans were dashed.

"When you left the Air Force, you came back to the University of Washington where you graduated with degrees in both Chinese and Japanese. And while you were going to school, you studied alongside Bruce Lee, which I imagine was a cool side benefit. Was he headed for the movies then?"

"Yeah. That was his goal."

"What was he like? He died so young."

"He was really focused, and proud of his physical health. He would never have done drugs, or hurt his body in any way."

"Didn't he die of a drug overdose?"

"That's what they say, but I don't believe it. At least, I can't believe it was self-inflicted. He was careful about his body, and real fussy about what he ate. He wouldn't even drink tea if it had caffeine."

"The big question I always had about your years of experience with the languages was why you just left all that and the possible career opportunities behind. Maybe you can fill me in on that. Why'd you just let it go?"

"There weren't that many opportunities back then," he said. "The Air Force tried to get me to re-up, but I didn't want that. Then, when I got my degrees, the government found out and wanted me to work for them in the CIA, or some other secret department, but the war was going on in Viet Nam and I didn't agree with that. The timing, I guess, wasn't right."

"The Air Force took up four years of your life when, it seems to me, you were getting into some kind of groove for wearing female clothing. I can't picture your time in the Air Force as giving you opportunities to dress up. How did you get by with denying this compulsion for four years?"

"It's not an all-consuming thing," he says.

Say what? This contradicts what he has said all along about cross-dressing being a compulsion that just builds and builds. But there's no point in challenging him. He's been very open with me so far, and if there is any one thing I've learned from this, it's that there are no logical explanations for compulsions. Compulsions just are.

"You could set it aside for four years?" I ask.

"For the most part," he says. "There was one time in Okinawa, when one of the guys in our squadron brought home a pair of panties as a trophy from one of his Tokyo R&R conquests, and it disappeared."

This makes me laugh. "Oh really?"

"I wore them a couple of times and then I thought I don't want to get caught with them on, so I ended up just throwing them out. Other than that ... and they say—and I don't know if it's true or not—that they put saltpeter in the food. Maybe, if they do, that's supposed to dull the sexual senses."

"When you joined the Air Force, did you make a conscious decision: 'I can't do this while I'm in the Air Force?'"

"Well. I don't know about that, but at any given time I can say, yes, I'm going to put on a dress, or no, I'm not going to. If the opportunities don't come up, they don't come up."

"So, proximity to women's clothes has a lot to do with following through, like when you're living in a house with women ..."

"Yeah. And I can think about it at night, you know. I can fantasize wearing a dress, without actually having to do it."

"You basically didn't wear women's clothing at all for four years. Since you didn't do that, did you pursue other sexual pleasures? Did you participate in any sexual pursuits on leave, like your buddies did?"

"A couple of times, I did," he said, "but not that much. It wasn't a moral thing. I just wasn't interested in hanging out with prostitutes. Although, hanging out in bars, I met some interesting people."

"Did you make any friends while you were in the Air Force?"

"There were five of us who hung out together at Yale, all of us studying Chinese. After we went through our year at Yale, we took the bus down to Texas where we went through three months of learning what we would be doing with our Chinese.

"One day, while the five of us were on the bus, we happened to be eating Three Musketeers candy bars. Somebody remembered that Three Musketeers sponsored Howdy Doody and Buffalo Bob, and we started calling each other Buffalo this and Buffalo that. We kept that up throughout our service days. Eventually, we became known as The Buffaloes and we formed sort of an exclusive club. We let everybody know it was exclusive and nobody else was allowed in. You know, when something becomes exclusive, then everybody wants in, especially if it's a social thing and you're looking for something to fill all the boring time of having to hang out with a bunch of guys with nothing else to do."

For some reason, it gives me comfort to know that Gene had real buddies and acted like a typical macho male; at least, while he was in the military. I guess that makes me no more high-minded than anyone else wanting to square their expectations with a familiar point of reference. Military man = macho male. My brother was a macho military male. And I call that comforting? Oh, dread.

Gene continues. "If somebody really wanted in, we would make him a chip."

"As in buffalo ch …?"

He looks at me like I'm a real dullard, and forges on. "But there could never be anyone but the original five Buffaloes. This was a big joke. But it got carried up. We had this commander who was almost afraid of us. He didn't quite know how to take us. We were all irreverent, but the Air Force had spent a lot of time and money training us in our specialty, and the military doesn't know how to deal with people like us, once we're trained. By the time we all got out of the Air Force, there was nobody any better than us at doing our job." He says this with suitable pride.

"You once told me about some kind of survival training you went through in the mountains of Nevada, but I didn't put much stock in it, because you tend to underplay everything you do. Then, there was a GI stationed in the Middle East a few years back who was shot down, or his plane crash-landed or something. I don't remember all the details, except he survived on his own in the desert and managed to avoid capture by the enemy for quite a long time. He eventually made his way into friendly territory and was rescued by our side. The explanation they gave for his surviving was that he got his training in the 'famous' Air Force survival training program in Nevada. Was that the same program you went through?"

"Yeah."

"Well, dammit! Tell me about it."

"It wasn't that big of a deal."

"Gene …" I say threateningly.

"They dropped us off in the mountains and it was our task to get ourselves back to the base without being captured. Of course, we knew we'd be captured. That was part of the training. But how long it would take, and what we had to go through to survive was the first test. So, as soon as we were dropped off, we started looking to find a way back."

"Did you have provisions … tent, food …?"

"No … we were simulating being lost unexpectedly. People don't prepare to be lost." Another look of infinite patience is sent my way.

"What did you eat?"

"Whatever we could find. Birds, bark, mushrooms, bugs…grasshoppers aren't bad when they're cooked … kind of crunchy, like …" He grins.

"Aw right, aw right! Continue, please." He knows I don't like creepy critters.

"Well, we got captured, as planned. And we were taught that once in captivity, it was our duty to escape, because brainwashing or torture sooner or later will work, so you have to get out before you give in.

"We started making up things to demonstrate to the enemy that we were sticking together. We'd find ways to harass our captors just enough to keep them off-balance and ourselves out of trouble. A couple of guys made an American flag out of a bunch of fabric scraps they gathered and put together. When they finished making the flag, they put it up in the main square of the compound, and we all gathered around it and started singing "The Star-Spangled Banner." It was pretty impressive. We all got in trouble when that happened."

"What kind of trouble?"

"They isolated us and put us into separate little cages that were just big enough to hold us in sort of fetal positions. We couldn't stand up. They were dark and dirty and all that. And then eventually we were interrogated, one at a time."

"Were you afraid?"

"It got pretty real at times. The flag thing was real. You know I'm not that overtly patriotic, but that was real … it aroused some emotions."

"How long were you in the cage?"

"Oh, maybe a few days. It's hard to tell when it's dark all the time. One day, they came and got me and took me to another dark room. They sat me down on a little stool and put a bright light in front of me. It was shining right in my eyes so my pupils dilated and I could only see the shadows of my interrogators. I didn't answer their questions, so they started threatening me with a bunch of stuff. Finally, they asked me how I expected to get out of there if I didn't cooperate. I told them I expected to stand up and walk out the door that brought me in here."

"They must have laughed at that," I said.

"They thought it was pretty funny, then not so funny. One of them hit me and that pissed me off, so I got up off the stool and backed toward the door. Then I turned real fast—the door was open—and broke into a run out the door, across the compound, hit the woods, and escaped into friendly territory. I knew it wasn't far away. My captors were too startled to move. They were so sure I couldn't do what I said I was going to do, they didn't react quick enough to stop me."

"That was pretty gutsy. What made you think of that?"

"I couldn't think of any other way to get out of there, and even though they put me through some pretty tough moments, I knew I wouldn't be there indefinitely, and I knew they wouldn't kill me. There was nothing to lose by going for the most obvious solution. I figured I had a chance, so why not go for it."

"After Nevada, was it China?"

"Our mission was to spy on China, but we weren't stationed in China, of course. We were stationed in Okinawa. It was a kind of screwy setup. We had both the Chinese and the Russian linguists at our base. We were in what was called Security Services. The planes we flew in weren't connected to us. They belonged to another unit, and it was their job to fly us. But they weren't allowed into where we were because they weren't cleared.

"It would have been all right if all the Russian linguists were transferred to northern Japan so they could fly out of there. And if the Chinese linguists could fly out of Okinawa, we'd be centrally located to fly our missions off the coast of China. On paper it made sense, except the planes we flew in on our missions were not under our command. They were stationed in Japan.

"To fly our missions, we had to fly with one crew from Okinawa to Central Japan, under one command. Then to get on the right command plane for missions, we'd fly on another plane with another crew out of Japan. Then our original flight crew would fly their command plane back to Okinawa without us. When our mission was complete, another crew under our command would fly to Japan from Okinawa, to return us to Okinawa. It meant extra crews and longer flights, but that was the military, and the first order of business was not to make sense; it was to protect individual commands.

"There was one Friday I noticed that a mission was scheduled to fly out of Okinawa, and there was nobody scheduled in the position I normally would fill. So, I put myself on it and went to Japan for a few days. When I got back, my friends were waiting for me and they told me I better watch out. 'They're ticked off at you," they said. But they couldn't do anything even if they were ticked off, because if they did anything, they'd have to explain why the plane was scheduled to leave without a linguist on it. So, technically, I did them a favor by hopping a ride."

"Glad to hear you're protecting the backsides of our military brass," I comment sarcastically.

"Another time, one of the Buffaloes wanted to see his girlfriend in Japan. He took some leave. The way it worked was, you could catch a hop on a military plane if there was space available and you weren't scheduled on a mission. But, to leave, you had to officially sign out, and when you returned, you'd have to sign back in. He wasn't sure he could get a hop and he didn't want to sign out if he couldn't get on one. The planes and pilots weren't always there at the base waiting for us, so the deal was he would go down to the field to fly out, and if he didn't come right back, I would go sign him out.

"The first couple of nights he didn't get the hop and he came back. The third night he did get on, and I forgot to sign him out. Everybody knew he was out on leave, but they didn't know he hadn't signed out.

"While he was out, the Cuban missile crisis broke out, and they sent bulletins for everybody to come back to base. A special bulletin went to Japan to get him back, but when they found out he hadn't signed out, they couldn't let him sign back in. They were going to court martial him for not signing out, except they would have had to explain why he'd been gone for a week before they knew he hadn't signed out. So, they decided to just let it go."

I'm listening to Gene talk about his military experience just like any GI I'd ever heard relating his experiences. Again, I am thinking that Gene is a regular guy, with regular buddies, sharing regular experiences. His clothing preferences are neither a part of, nor a party to, any description one would have said about him. So why is it such a big deal? It would seem that clothes don't make the man.

An interesting side note here is that, in doing my research to better understand cross-dressing, I came across a reference that says heterosexual cross-dressers are disproportionately represented among the retired military. Many of them apparently joined to assure themselves of their masculinity. They used the uniforms to put their masculine fears to rest and hide their feminine side. This was not the case with Gene. He joined because he had always dreamed of flying airplanes—but it's an interesting study just the same.

"Were your missions dangerous?" I ask.

"Not from anything the Chinese would do."

"Really! What do you mean by that?"

"Well, I remember one time we were taking off and the guys up front noticed that the windshield was cracked, so we had to return to base and change planes. A week later, as we took off in the same plane, the windshield blew out. They hadn't gotten around to fixing it. This time we had to make an emergency landing.

"And there was another time we sort of got lost. We weren't supposed to fly over China. We didn't have to, because we were up high enough that we could hear their messages a long way inland. We were supposed to be flying along the coast. I went back to get some coffee in the galley in the back of the plane. I was standing with my coffee, looking out the window and I saw land below us. We were supposed to be flying over ocean. Land meant we were flying over China, which was definitely a violation of international treaties. I called up front to the cockpit, and we made a hasty retreat. The navigator was completely lost. But at least he now knew he was lost, so he called the base to get directions to get us back on course."

"What if the Chinese had discovered you were flying over their country?"

"There would have been an international incident and we'd have been fucked, both by the Chinese and the American governments. Under those circumstances, we would have been completely on our own.

"There was another time I remember. We left Okinawa to fly to Clark Air Force Base, near Manila. We always knew where we were going, but the flight crew never did. They were supposed to follow what they call coordinates. Our navigator was trying to find the coordinates to show him where he was supposed to land. He couldn't find them, so he couldn't find where we were supposed to land. We knew it was to be the Philippines, but he was flying somewhere near Guam, which was 2,000 miles away from our real destination. Incidents like that caused us to not have a lot of confidence in the training and follow-through on our side."

"Did the flight crew ever resent not knowing what you were doing?"

"They probably knew what we were doing, generally. They just didn't know the specifics. They didn't know what our equipment looked like—we were responsible for that—but they probably knew what we were doing with it."

"Dad was sick while you were gone, but you were home when he had his heart surgery and they found the cancer. I remember having lunch with you in the café near the hospital thinking he would be in surgery for several hours, and we looked up and saw Mom walking toward us, after about an hour and a half. She had special permission to watch the surgery. Seeing her so soon, we knew something wasn't right. She sat down and told us they closed him up because he was full of cancer and there was no point in continuing the heart surgery. How was it that you were there?"

"I was home on special leave. The Red Cross arranged it."

"That was in April," I recall. "Then you went back and you were called home again in August. How did that work? What did they say?"

"They called me in and said my dad was not doing so good, so I needed to go home. I knew when I went back to the missions in April, I'd probably be called home again."

"You got home in time to spend a few days with us before he died. Do you remember those days?"

"Sort of."

"He was kind of in-and-out of comas, or dreams. He dreamed out loud about family trips we used to take to California when we were kids. It was like going back to those times. He said, 'Look Ma, this motel has a pink room. I think we better stay here tonight.' Mom always liked pink rooms. She said that would be fine, and he grinned. And we all laughed as if his story was going on right then, like we were kids again, traveling with Mom and Dad. It was a few good days for us, even though we were losing him. And, after the funeral, you returned to your missions. Did it feel odd, leaving like that?"

"Not really. I was prepared. I knew when I went home the second time, he'd probably die before I returned."

"When you got out, did you immediately start wearing dresses again? Was it like a pent-up release thing, or did you gradually get back into it?"

"It was somewhat immediate. It was probably about then that I bought my first clothes on my own. There was a ten cents store at our junction, and I went there and stood around hemming and hawing and mumbling, and ended up buying a pair of panties. I don't remember what excuses I had, or what I said, or anything."

"Because I no longer lived there and my chest of drawers was not available?"

He ignores me.

"And there were a couple of times I went out and bought dresses. I went to White Center and some other places. I'd try to get out of the immediate area of where we lived. I think I still had some of your old stuff stashed, too. You had a petticoat that was made out of red taffeta. I had that for a while and some other thing of yours, too."

"When you came back to the U.S.," I said, "you lived for a while with Mom. Lloyd and I were back from Alaska by then and starting our family, so I was closer in touch with what was going on in our family.

"One day, Mom made you leave her house. She told me you were hanging out with a lot of 'Orientals,' she called them, and she thought you were dating a Japanese girl. She still had some feelings left over from her brothers fighting Japan during World War II. Was her explanation real, or was it a cover for other reasons, like she knew you were dressing up?" I ask.

"I don't remember for sure," he says. "It probably was some of that—the friends I had—and some other reasons. She helped me find an apartment in the U District and she paid for that."

"Yeah," I say, with more than a little chagrin. "She picked up your dirty laundry, brought it home, washed it, and returned it to you. And I know she bought your groceries, too. Some kind of way to kick someone out."

"I was going to school at the U at the time," he says. "After a while, I moved back into her house again and I went shopping a few times from her place. There was a Penney's downtown and they were open late on Friday nights, and there weren't many people shopping at that time of day. I remember I bought a real nice red slip at The Bon Marché and they asked me if I had panties to match, and I did.

"The pink A-line skirt I was wearing when I wanted to talk to Mom, I don't remember when or how I got that. I do know it was from Sears. I think it was from the catalog, but I don't remember ordering it. It would have had to come to her house.

"Then I remember the day when Uncle Dick had his cancer scare. I traveled over to Yakima on a Greyhound bus. I had on the red half slip and panties and nylons under my regular clothes and I kept kicking myself for having done that. Here I was stuck on a bus to eastern Washington not knowing what could happen."

It sounds like Gene had no trouble making the transition from the excitement of uniformed reconnaissance flights in the Far East, off the coast of China, to the thrill of riding a Greyhound bus from Seattle to Yakima in a half slip and panties. In fact, the look on his face when he recalls these things indicates that a bus ride to Yakima excited him far more than flying across the ocean on a mission for the U. S. government.

I asked him if he kept in touch with his fellow Buffaloes.

"No" was all he said.

It was a brief and final farewell to Team Buffalo.

Chapter Eleven

TAKING RISKS
Night walks and close encounters

"Gene, you mentioned a while back that you would take late-night walks all dressed up. I wasn't ready to hear about it then. It sounded so dangerous; it gave me the creeps. Why at night? Did you do it for the danger? Did you get off on the risks involved?"

"I did it at night because I didn't want to get caught."

"That's all?"

"The first time I could go outside with women's clothes on was after I graduated from the UW, and had started working for Sears. I moved out of Mom's house into an apartment in Lake City. That apartment was on the ground floor and had a front and back door, and at night I could go outside with women's clothes on. But I didn't go far. I just hung around the back door and that was as far as I felt I could go, living there.

"Then I moved across the street from Sick's Seattle Stadium, and that's where I did my first real cruising at night, actually walking outside in the middle of the night."

"Oh, my God! That was a rough part of town, mixed races, pockets of poverty, and identity struggles in the late sixties and early seventies. That was dangerous!"

"I moved there so I could watch the baseball games from my balcony. I didn't think about the other stuff."

That would go with his linear thinking. Focus on what it is that you want, and go there. Don't entertain any reasons for not doing what you want. But holy crap!

Sometimes you have to consider possible consequences, don't you?

He continues. "I wasn't sure if it was legal to wear women's clothes or not, and I wanted to find out, in case I got caught. I didn't want to get arrested and end up with a picture of me in the paper, sharing a cell with some Bubba who would make me his wife. I looked up the phone number of the Vice Department of the Seattle Police Department and called them. When the guy answered the phone, it was about midnight. He answered, 'Homicide'. I asked for Vice and he said after regular business hours all calls go through to homicide. I asked him what the law was and he said, 'Go for it, if you want.'"

"Really! That's an odd response. Maybe he was a cross-dresser. I read in a book that cross-dressers will tell you they became a cop, a firefighter, joined the military, and so forth; jobs that require uniforms, to hide their true natures. Wearing the uniforms gave them a masculine façade. I think the book was called *Normal* by Amy Bloom. Anyway, what happened next?"

"So I began to take midnight walks. I'd wait until late at night when there were fewer people out and about. I'd stick to the side street with less traffic. In the dark, I could see car's headlights in plenty of time to find some cover. It was only eight or ten blocks from my place to the lake, and there was a big park on the way. I could walk through the middle of that park when it was dark. I'd do that every once in a while."

"You're creeping me out. That's how people get killed, doing weird things under the supposed cover of dark parks at night. You were wearing a coat, right? Your women's clothing wasn't visible, was it?"

"It was visible."

"Oh, sweet Jesus! I don't want to hear this. Did anything bad happen?"

"Well, my walks were in the middle of the night and I avoided people. But one night I went out wearing a favorite suit of mine. It was a dusty pink/ burgundy houndstooth check. The skirt had two inverted pleats, and it had a matching waist length, long-sleeved jacket. I wore a white ruffled blouse again, white anklets, and flat shoes. Underneath I had on my usual bra, slip, and panties.

"I was walking along, when suddenly a cop car pulled up and stopped me. Two officers got out and came up to me. I knew I wouldn't be arrested, but I was afraid I might be taken in for questioning, and then released to get home on my own. When they started questioning me on the spot, I felt a sense of relief. It actually felt good to stand there dressed in women's clothes having a conversation with two strangers. It was as if the world had finally gotten it right.

"They took down my name and address and asked a few questions about myself, such as who I was, what I did for a living, and what I was doing out in the middle of the night. I answered as best as I could, and they were apparently satisfied.

"At the conclusion of the questioning, one of them asked me if I was wearing panties under my skirt. When I said yes, they both wanted to see. Mothers always tell you to wear clean underwear in case someone sees it. I was totally prepared. I was wearing pink nylon panties with panels of lace down each side in front. They were my prettiest and most feminine panties, and I was absolutely delighted to show them off. I lifted up my skirt and gave them their look. They went away very happy, and I was probably the topic of discussion around the water cooler for a while.

"I was on cloud nine walking home. I took the busiest and brightest street, ready to be seen by one and all who might pass by. It felt so good to dress up as a woman in front of others that at that point I began to think of being a cross-dresser—not as a curse, but as a blessing."

"You stood in the middle of the park and pulled your dress up? I guess they were worried about whether you would expose yourself if you lifted your skirt."

"No, I think they were just curious. Something they could laugh about to their buddies back at the station."

"Were you afraid when they stopped you?"

"Initially I was, but it was like every time I got caught. There's fear, immediately followed by resignation. And I think inside, all along, I wanted to get caught. I think I wanted to be discovered."

"That's quite a story! I'm glad that particular encounter turned out well. But I keep thinking there had to be something that made you keep tempting fate."

"I think it was that feeling of wanting to be discovered, over a period of years, that finally led to October 11th, here."

"Why do you think you wanted to be discovered?" I ask.

"Oh, partly it has to do with wanting to be punished, or embarrassed. And part of it is getting it off my chest; getting it out in the open for relief. And, ultimately, although mostly it's wishful thinking, I think I am hoping for acceptance.

"Another time I remember was when you were living on Sylvester Road. I stayed with you for a while, and I had some clothes there. What I'd do is wear a slip and panties with a T-shirt over them. One night after dark, I was going to go out for a walk and I started walking and I got halfway down the driveway, and a couple of the Bradley girls came out on the other side of the hedge. It was dark and I don't know if they saw me or not. I went back in the house really quick."

"You moved to Bellingham from that house. You stayed with Jack and Shelley for a while, until you found a job and a place of your own. Did you wear female clothing while you stayed with them?"

"Actually, Shelley was living in Seattle and going to school. The only time I wore clothes at Jack's house was when the Southfork Bluegrass Band, that Jack played in, would be out of town on a gig or something, and I would dress up then. There was one time when I might have been caught. I'd fallen asleep and the band got back before I woke up and went upstairs to my room. I was asleep in the music room, and there were no lights on. I woke up to hear Jack say, 'Don't go in there. Gene's sleeping.' But whether he saw me or not, I don't know."

"I bet he did," I respond, "and if he did, he wouldn't have mentioned it. I have a certain respect for him. I don't know why. I think he's pretty accepting. How'd you get out of that situation?"

"They jammed for a while in the living room and they all finally went to bed, and I did too. Shortly after that I got a job, the same one I have now, and I moved to my own apartment. Then I could dress up whenever I felt like it. That's when I started getting clothes out of the Sears catalog.

"One of the problems of ordering by mail is you don't know if it's going to fit, and if it doesn't, you're stuck. Another problem, if you order two things that are supposed to go together and they're out of one of the items, you end up with something that doesn't match with anything else. The dress I was wearing the first time with you, I got that through the catalog.

"Sears was easier than Penney's. You could order by mail. Penney's orders you had to phone in, and they would know because of the man's voice. But Sears got out of the catalog business."

"Why do you think they would know just because you are buying the clothes that you would be wearing the clothes? Men do buy clothes for women."

"Yeah," he acknowledged, "but not without a lot of tee-heeing afterwards by the salespeople. And then in Bellingham, not two or three times a week, but maybe two or three times a year, I would go out for a walk in the middle of the night. Or take a drive. When I'd leave my place, I would get almost completely dressed, with pants on and stuff, and then I'd drive out somewhere and pull over and finish getting dressed. But it was kind of a hassle to reverse the action and get the dress off. So, when I went out, I would time it so I'd arrive back home at three o'clock in the morning.

"That was when I started carrying clothes with me whenever I'd make a trip to Seattle to watch some of my friends play music at the New Melody, or somewhere else. They'd finish playing at two o'clock and I'd drive someplace dark and change into the clothes and drive back to Bellingham, getting to my place about three in the morning. And I'd just get out of the car and go inside.

"I remember a particular trip I took a few nights before Shannon's wedding. There was some banjo-playing down in Pendleton, Oregon, which is about 320 miles southeast of Seattle. I happened to be on vacation that week, so I decided I'd drive down there to see that.

"I left my place about midnight and drove there to somewhere between Ellensburg and Yakima, wearing a skirt and blouse, where I found a wide spot in the road to sleep. That was when I had the pickup with a canopy. I got in the back and slept there, then changed out of the skirt in the morning and went the rest of the way in regular clothes. I was going to stay the next night at Uncle Jack's in Milton-Freewater, but Jenny happened to be there, and then Aunt Lide came over.

"I mentioned that I was going to see some bluegrass people in Pendleton and they wanted to go with me, so I couldn't dress up again until I was on my way back home when the music was done. I gassed up, went to a parking lot, and changed back into the blouse and skirt. I drove until I found a rest stop and went around to where there were no cars, and I got out and walked a bit. People could probably see me from a distance, but I knew they wouldn't be able to tell what I was wearing."

"Gene, I think I can sense there's more than one reason why you put on the clothes. One reason, naturally, would be the sexual rush, but you could get that at home by yourself. But this going out in public, there's got to be more to it. Whether you admit it or not, it's just plain dangerous, the way you do it."

"The sexual rush is one of the benefits," he responds," "but it's not the only reason. The real reason is just that I love being in them, being in girlish things, that is. Sexual pleasure can be derived if I want it to, but there's more to it than that."

"It seems to me that you take a lot of risks, but you've been lucky, so I shouldn't fret over what hasn't happened to you. However, I'm your sister and I worry just the same."

"Well, yeah. But this is not something I do a lot. It's only a few times a year," he says.

"If you were discovered by yourself at night, hiding behind a tree or something, don't you think that it would be more suspicious than if you were seen walking on a public street during the day?" I ask.

"If you're on a public street during the day, you're going to be discovered," he says, making my remarks sound incredibly stupid. "But if you play your cards right, you're not apt to be discovered at night. If you're reasonably cautious—which I am—you won't be. And at night, it's dark and you can hide."

"Do you like hiding?"

"No, but it's preferable to being caught."

I'll leave it at that. Gene's nightly adventures still give me the creeps. He's playing with fate —bad fate—and that kind of fate eventually wins.

"Halloween of '95 was the first time I wasn't wearing any men's clothes at all. I thought if someone were to see me, they would think I was just decked out for Halloween. I wore a red tunic thing and a bobbysoxer kind of skirt. Actually, it was a Halloween costume dress for a girl, but it wouldn't fit so I got some scissors and cut it off above the elastic part at the waist, and it worked as a skirt. Then I put on a witch's cape and hat and went out as the Bobbysoxer from Hell.

"I parked my car across the street that night so I wouldn't have to walk back around and maybe run into my neighbors. I put on all the clothes and makeup. Then I got into the car and drove across town to a McDonald's and went through their line to get some dinner. Then I drove back through town and stopped where I had to get out of my car and drop off my light bill. After that, I went driving again until about ten o'clock and I still wasn't quite ready to quit, so I got out of the car and went for a walk. I walked for about an hour.

"The last part of the walk, I took off the cape because I got tired of screwing with it, and my hose kept running down my legs, and I got tired of dealing with that, so I stopped to pull them back up. A girl came by about the time I stood up. She said hello and I said hello back. She probably was surprised to hear my voice. I don't know what she thought. I just kept walking. That was my one-and-only walk in prime time.

"It was about a week after that when I fell and broke my elbow. I was wearing a dress then too, but it was late. I'd gone to get my mail and I fell off the steps to my apartment.

"It was about two o'clock in the morning, and I was tempted to go to the hospital that way. But there were two things that kept me from doing that. One, it was two a.m. and I wasn't sure I could get it taken care of and back home before daylight. The other thing was, by then I hadn't bought any new clothes for a long time. Everything I had was getting seedy and real ratty, and I wanted to be dressed better than that if I was going to come out. But I was real tempted to go anyway.

"Then I had what I call a 'Mitty Moment.' You remember Walter Mitty, the milquetoast fictional guy that James Thurber wrote about. Walter Mitty sat in his chair and dreamed up stuff he wouldn't do in real life. I imagined what it would be like lying there on a gurney at the hospital in a dress while I was getting my arm set. My Mitty Moments kept my fantasies in perspective. They helped me avoid doing really stupid things.

"Do you want to hear some of my Mitty Moments?"

I'm totally wrung out from hearing about Gene's nighttime adventures. But I'll try to stay awake and listen.

"Yeah, tell me more."

SHIRLEY ANNE THOM

Chapter Twelve

MITTY MOMENTS
Fantasies relieve loneliness

"They start out really simple, just some things I sit and daydream about. Most of them are inspired by something that either happened to me or something I read about.

"One example would be thinking about how it would be on Halloween in a girl's costume instead of a boy's, wondering what that would be like. I'd start with the idea and embellish it as I went along.

"In my Mitty Moment, I would decide the day before Halloween to wear a girl's costume to go trick-or-treating. Everybody would kid me about dressing like a girl. It would start out that way, and then it expanded to where it wasn't just for trick-or-treating. There would be a party at school and I could dress up all day. It went from that to where Halloween was on Saturday and the school party was on Friday, so I could get to do it for two days. Then it became a whole weekend and it just goes on. Finally, it got to the point where I could get by with that for one Halloween, but the next year people might ask questions.

"And it went on to a new moment where I don't know if I had just you as a sister, or I had three sisters, or two girls were living with us and the way we decided who got to be what on Halloween was that everybody wrote on a piece of paper what we wanted to wear, and Mom would put our papers in a hat and we'd draw the papers from a hat. The odds were three-to-one that I would get to wear a girl's outfit. But because of the situation, I wouldn't be blamed if I had to wear a girl's outfit. Nobody would know."

"Then that means you would have to put in a boy's outfit," I say, "or they would know."

"The ultimate version would be where all four of us ended up in girls' outfits."

Laughing, I say, "So you didn't put the choice of a boy's outfit in the hat."

Ignoring me, he says, "That was one Mitty. Another one was based on a boy being a girl movie star, with a wig and everything, and I'd imagine myself in that role. And then I decided it would be easier going through makeup each day if I just wore girls' stuff all the time and we wouldn't have to spend so much time in the makeup department.

"And that expanded to where Mom was a stage mother-type and there was an audition coming up in two weeks to cast the role, and she decided the movie plot wouldn't fly unless the boy who was chosen could make himself up to be a convincing girl. Otherwise, nobody would believe he was getting away with his disguise. So, she spent time from then on teaching me how to act like a girl.

"I would show up at the audition as a girl, and sit in the waiting room among all those boys wanting to audition. When it was my turn to go into the audition room, they'd look at me and say, 'We're sorry. This part is for a boy.' I'd take off the wig and surprise them, and I'd get the part. Then I'd get to spend all the time during the entire shooting of the film as a girl.

"I remember one summer reading about a judge sentencing a couple of juvenile delinquents to wear girls' clothes. I imagined myself doing some minor infraction to get myself in front of that judge, and get sentenced to being a girl for a month. That evolved to me being taken to a store and getting fitted into my sentencing garments."

"Do you ever get sexually aroused in your Mitty Moments?" I don't know why I put that in there. But sometimes the sexual overtones of his wanting to wear women's clothing are hard to ignore. It's the most difficult part of the acceptance of cross-dressing. I really don't want to hear about my brother's sexual fantasies, or to be a part of them in any way.

"In those days I probably would have, but you know I'm getting older," he says, and then he moves along.

When he gets on a particular subject, there's no deterring him. And right now, we're into Mitty Moments.

"Mom told me once that she and Dad had talked about putting me in a military school," he says.

"Why?"

"Probably to get me out of their hair. Dealing with me had to be hard on them. I started imagining what it would be like to go away to school. The first thing I thought about was, they might have a school play and they would have to have someone play the girl, because military schools were not coed. I thought I could get to do that.

"Then I combined that scenario with the judge in my other moment. He could have said, 'Your punishment is to be assigned to a boys' school and you have to be dressed as a girl.' Then I'd go off on several variations of that.

"In one variation they knew why I was being put in there, and because they knew I liked to wear girls' clothes, they tried to break me of the habit by forcing me to wear girls' clothes all the time.

"When I watch movies, sometimes I identify with the girls in them. *The Bad Seed* always comes to my mind. I think the director of that movie must have been a cross-dresser. Because of the way it was staged, every move she made seemed like she was teaching me how to do it; how it would feel to be like her. In one scene there was kind of a crazy guy who was the housekeeper. When she was leaving to go to school, the crazy guy decided to throw water at her, and where the camera angle was you could partially see up her dress. When she jumped as the water hit her, you could see all the way up. I felt like they designed this movie to suit me. Some of my Mitty Moments had me acting that out.

"In some of my Mitty Moments I would just get caught. Like I'd fall asleep in a dress and not wake up in time to avoid getting caught. I'd wake up and someone would be there, standing over me.

"And some moments involved Mom laying a trap for me. She decided she wanted to catch me at it, so she would pretend she was leaving for the whole day and then she would come back to find me in her clothes. She would have a set of clothes in her closet that were my size and she would make me change into those and say, 'Okay if you want to wear women's clothes, wear these.' In some moments, when I was wearing her dress, the doorbell would ring and I'd have to answer it."

• • • • •

"Would you like for that to really happen?" I ask.

"Probably. And then there were moments—you know she would always spank with a wooden spoon—when she would take me over her knee and make me pull up my dress. I think that had as much to do with, like I was telling you before—my theory that showing your panties was like baring your soul.

"A lot of guys will wear a dress for a joke, or for Halloween or a costume party, but they don't wear anything feminine underneath. By lifting the skirt up and showing the world that I am wearing the most intimate of girls' clothes … it's like you would be able to look and see me—the real me. Does that make any sense?"

Yes, it makes sense the way he tells it, but I don't like it. I don't like it one bit, and I'm not going to deal with it, although it does help me to understand the panties fetish. Panties are the symbol of his female focus. But they are no symbol for me. I don't need symbols. I don't have to wear silk panties to prove my femininity. And the thought of male gen … No. Like I said, I'm not going to deal with it. I don't have to, and I'm not going to. It's disgusting. I'm not going to deal with it. I'm going to alter this whole conversation.

"Do you have as many Mitty Moments, or fantasies, since you've come out?"

"Yes and no. I don't need as many. Like this weekend. If it were two years ago, I probably would have had one tonight. But now I don't need to. I've got the real thing.

"But when you mentioned the possibility a few weeks ago that you might have a Christmas party, that started me thinking about what that would be like.

"One version I came up with had me coming here first and getting dressed up and going over to Texie's house. But I don't know how we'd get from here to your car. We could probably take the stairs instead of the elevator. I would worry about embarrassing you in front of your neighbors. But as far as going over there and getting out of the car, that wouldn't be a problem, unless Texie would be embarrassed by it and wouldn't want her neighbors to know.

"And that moment evolved from the Christmas party to opening presents on Christmas Eve."

"Has there been a down side to coming out?"

"Only like I've already said. It's the feeling that I've let you down, and knowing that I've put a lot of stuff into your lap that you probably could live without."

"This letting me down," I say, laughing. "When did you get the idea that you were ever on some big pedestal that you'd have to come down from?"

"I never thought of myself in terms of being on a pedestal," he responds.

"Well, you're not. And that's the point. Neither am I. So, this letting people up and down feels a bit strange. Did you ever think there might be more differences between girls and boys than differences between men and women?

Girls and boys are acting out roles they think they've observed, and play-acting involves exaggeration."

"Part of it could be that when I grew up men were supposed to be the strong ones and initiate everything, and maybe that's where I got the sense that it might be easier being a girl. I don't know how much sense there is to that."

"It makes no sense to me. It's a bunch of macho crap. Women are the care-givers. Everyone knows that."

"But what I remember was the norm when I was growing up," he says.

"So, if you were a boy today, you think some things might be different."

"Last spring," he notes, "when some school was trying to install dress codes, two or three boys wore dresses in protest. Their pictures were in some papers. That never would have happened when we were growing up. And if I'd grown up now, all this coming out and everything probably wouldn't have happened the same. I'd probably be a hairdresser."

"Did you ever think of choosing a profession that would make your cross-dressing easier? A lot of your Mitty Moments involved acting. Did you ever think of doing that?"

"No."

"Why?"

"Because then everyone would know for sure."

"And you don't want people to know."

"Not yet," he says. "And I've never wanted to call a lot of attention to myself, which you have to do if you're acting. The hairdressing, too, I would distance myself from doing that too. People would figure it out."

"Texie's hairdresser showed up for work one day as a woman. Would that feel neat?"

"Yeah, it would. And if I had my life to do over, it might be different. But see, I had to live with the times and influences I grew up with."

I'm trying to imagine how different it would be if we were born to this world, rather than the world that existed when we were born, and I can't say with confidence that it would be different. In fact, I don't think it would be. People are still sexually phobic.

I don't think it's one thing so much, like cross-dressing, or being gay. It's anything that's different. People are so insecure about their sexuality. Hell, when you hear that a book says healthy people should have sexual intercourse three times a week, those that have less than that worry that they're undersexed, and those who have more begin to think they're perverted.

People don't know what is "normal," so they imagine anything other than what they know or do might be more than they can handle. They put what's different from their personal experience into the pervert column so they can ignore it, make fun of it, or try to stop it.

Things are beginning to change, and we try to tell ourselves it's getting better. But is it really? Sadly, I don't think it would be that much different if Gene and I were born today. Maybe Mom would be more able to cope, because she would have more people to talk to about it. Talking helps. I sure as hell hope that talking helps. I want it to help. That's why we are talking.

Chapter Thirteen

HE WANTS US TO BE SISTERS
Girly sisters

Gene's every waking moment seems to be consumed with viewing, touching, and talking about clothes, but we're done reminiscing so much. We've returned to living in the present. And it's getting tougher, rather than easier, for me to handle our new relationship. It's becoming too overwhelming for me to try to understand this anymore.

My brother's clothing fetish is so all-consuming; he is lost to me underneath a pathetic pile of garish clothes. Although I've tried to influence his choices, it's the bright colors and showy patterns that still attract most of his attention.

We're forever focused on his clothing stash, and I'm sick of it. He counts and catalogues his panties, for God's sake! His mind keeps a virtual diary of when he wore what pair of panties with what dress, and for what occasion. It's purple for Huskies' football days; teal for Mariners' baseball evenings; lavender for Easter; red for Christmas. Where does it end? Brown for Thanksgiving? Oh, wretch!

But today is another shopping day. Lingerie is on sale, and we're right here in the middle of it, taking our places around the many pretties. The shopping for Mom charade is history. Let people talk, if they want to. A sale is a sale, and the commissioned salespeople are happy we're spending money. We spend it, and they earn it. If they snicker after we're gone, so be it. We don't care.

Gene has bought himself another gross of panties. When we arrive home, he takes every pair of these treasures out of the bag, holds them up, and describes each one of them to me, as if I can't see them myself.

"I got these two lavender ones, and this one with pink roses, and this one with yellow flowers, and look at this! I've been looking for just the right shade of teal to wear to Mariners games. I got two of these so I can wear one on Saturday, and the other one on Sunday.

"When the Mariners were in the playoffs for the first time back in '95, I had this pair of light teal-colored panties I would change into to wear to those games. I have a pair of light purple that I always wear to the Huskies games. It was about that time in '95, I got the idea there was no need to change clothes to go to the games. I could wear panties all the time instead of shorts, so I quit wearing men's shorts altogether. You know the old story of your mother always saying you should wear clean underwear in case you get in an accident. Now I always have clean underwear in every shade I need. Getting two pairs of panties in the Mariners' shade of teal is a real score."

No pun intended, I hope. "For crying out loud, Gene, how many panties do you have?"

"Oh, I don't know," he says. "I guess about a hundred."

"A hundred?" I ask, incredulously. "I can't even imagine owning a hundred pair of panties. Don't you ever do a wash?"

"I just want my whole outfit to match," he answers.

Oh, Lordy, Lordy. I think I'll go to my room and read, or just go to bed. Sleep, more and more, serves as my escape hatch.

The first thing Gene says to me when I wake up in the morning and walk into the living room is, "I wrote them all down. I overestimated the number. I only have seventy-eight."

"Seventy-eight what?" I snap. I know perfectly well seventy-eight what. I'm just being ornery.

"Panties," he says. "I wrote them all down last night after you went to bed. I wanted to get it right. I have seventy-eight pairs of panties."

Someday I'll have the courage to tell Gene that panties are not something I care to discuss first thing Sunday morning, or care to discuss at all with my brother. Someday, I'll explain that I don't count panties with my daughters or my gal friends. I'll tell him we just don't do that. But I won't say anything now. I'll continue to hope that eventually he'll find other people who want to discuss underwear ad nauseam. Then I'll tell him that talking about underwear is not my idea of a satisfying weekend. But I can't go there now. Not when he's just become brave enough to talk about it with me. He's waited so long to share his feminine side that I can't risk his burying it again. I'll just change the subject.

"So, Gene. I got a card from you a couple of days ago. It was all flowery and cute, with the bunnies and all. In it you wrote that you wanted me to think of you as the sister I never had. What does that mean?"

"I don't know," he says. "Just pretend I'm a girl—like you."

"But you're not a girl like me. You're a man, a male person."

I might as well forge ahead and finish what's on my mind. Over the past few weeks, Gene's point of reference is all about being a girl. He never says woman.

"And, in fact, Gene, I'm not a girl 'like me' either. I'm not a girl at all. I'm a woman. Why do you say girl rather than woman?"

"Maybe it's because I started thinking about being a girl when I was a boy and I never adjusted."

"Okay, I can understand that, but you know it's kind of irritating. I haven't thought like a girl since I was a girl, and I have no desire to try to recapture what I may have been thinking a half-century ago. I've been a woman for a long time, and I like being a woman. I like being a grown-up. So, let's forget the girl thing. What do you think we grown-up females do that you'd like to know more about?"

"That's something I was sort of hoping to find out from you," he says. "To me, it would be fun to go out with you and Texie … or maybe not out. Maybe just hang out here together."

Texie is our cousin. We're both close to Texie. She could be my sister, a sister I could relate to. She's a modern woman. I can see us as sisters. I can't see Gene as my sister. He's too silly. A few weeks back he said girls are frivolous, and he'd like to know what it feels like to be frivolous. Maybe some girls are frivolous, but my sister wouldn't be frivolous. If she were, I wouldn't like her. And besides, she'd be a grown woman by now. And the women I relate to are not frivolous. Fun, yes. Frivolous, no.

"I told Texie about you."

"What did she say?" he asks.

"Not much. She said she wouldn't say anything to you or anyone else until you said it's okay for her to know. As you can imagine, she's very supportive. Is it okay that I told her?"

"Yeah, I guess. You shouldn't have to keep this burden to yourself."

"For now, Gene, I'll forget you said 'burden.' That offends me. What I'd really like to know more about is how you think men and women are different. Do you think our differences are deep and innate, or more surface and learned?"

"I don't think so much on that level."

"You want to know about our surface affectations and presentations. Is that right?"

"I have some theories about clothes that just seem to make sense to me," he says.

"So, we're back to clothes," I say. "Why isn't there more?"

"Clothes are a reflection of who we are," he says, "and women's clothes have a deeper effect on your personality than you know, or will admit to. For instance, women's hemlines go up or down, depending on age. Have you noticed that? If Rebecca and Rachael and Lora were all wearing the same dress, the hems would measure the same from the ground up. If they stood next to each other, the hems would line up."

"Yes, dress hems are sometimes measured from the floor up. And, sometimes, when minis are in, they are measured from the knees up. What's your point, Gene?"

"At the same distance from the ground, or floor, on Rebecca (adult), a dress would come to just below her knees; on Rachael (teenager) it would probably be above her knees, and for Lora (age eight) it would be up higher. And, if you're like, say, a two-year-old, it would barely cover your panties. So, you have little girls walking around exposing their most intimate parts."

"That's just bull shit," I respond immediately. "Hems are measured from the ground up on each person, and according to current styles. Knees would be two feet from the ground up on each person, and according to current styles, knees would be two feet from the floor on Rebecca, eighteen inches on Rachael, and twelve inches for Lora. They wouldn't line up the way you are imagining it. And while women's styles change and hems go up and down, little girl styles, for the most part, are consistent: straight skirts go below the knees, puffy skirts end above the knees."

This is just another silly discussion, until he says, "The most intimate part of your body is exposed for the whole world to see at an age—three-to-five—when you start to form ideas. Seems like that could have a long-term psychological effect. It's like having a window into your soul, a look inside you, and the whole world sees it, starting when you're very young. I don't know if that makes any sense to you."

Oh, my God! I am TOTALLY ill-equipped to deal with this turn. Is my brother some kind of voyeur? Or is this the real explanation as to why he keeps saying girl instead of woman? He's telling me about his impressions of feminine attire formed when he was about three or four. He's telling me that peeking at panties gave him a sexual rush because he was imagining the body underneath; the body that holds the secret to feeling feminine. That's why the panties fetish. This is a disgusting revelation. I'm repulsed.

"So, you formed this theory all on your own—that little girls expose their souls?"

"It just makes sense to me."

"Well, it makes no sense to me, and frankly you're giving me the creeps again. Do you still get a thrill peeking at little girls' panties?"

His response is swift and adamant.

"I don't get a thrill that way. I'm not interested in little girls. As a boy, I noticed panties on little girls because they are exposed on little girls. It made me curious because women cover their panties up. They are always making a point of pulling their dresses down when they sit, so they don't expose anything.

(Well, DUH!)

"The thrill for me comes from feeling panties on me, against my body, not seeing them on someone else. It was just a curiosity thing when I was a kid because I noticed that your panties were different from my shorts. That's all."

I'm going to accept his explanation because to not accept it would mean I could NOT accept Gene. And I do believe him. He has shown no signs ever—and I do mean ever—of having any kind of prurient interest in little girls. Nevertheless, I'm going to move away from this and get back to adult sisterhood. That's what I'm trying to figure out this weekend.

"Let's get back to your wanting to experience the imagined art of sisterhood with me. Is that all right?"

"Yeah."

"Quit saying 'yeah.' I want better answers. I want to know how you imagine that men are different from women. I want to know what you think the differences are between the conversations that men have with men and women have with women."

Again, he doesn't hear my words. He hears only my voice, and he responds when the voice stops.

"I think I can relate more on the level of girls rather than women," he says, "because, as I said, I formed my impressions back then. I can't relate so well to women, especially older women. I see those foundations and stuff and I can't see how they could wear all that."

He keeps going back to clothes, as if they define all things. I ask about conversations and he answers about clothes. He thinks older women wear foundations, and he doesn't want to wear foundations, and therefore he can't relate to older women. But he can relate to girls because they wear pink fluffy dresses and he wants to wear pink fluffy dresses. Never mind the rest of their beings, or his, for that matter. And who wears foundations anymore, anyway?

"I think I qualify as an older woman," I say, "and I don't know what the hell you're talking about. What foundations and stuff?"

"Oh, I've seen pictures…"

"When, Gene? See, or saw? Was it yesterday, or forty years ago?"

"It was a while back."

"That's what I thought. I think most of your perceptions represent a generational gap rather than a gender gap. Grown men and women, conversation-wise, are not that different today. Yeah, women talk about their kids and families, but so do men. And, believe me, some of the conversations women have about other things—like, for instance, sex—can get just as raunchy as anything you've ever heard, or overheard, from men.

"But," I add, trying to bring it back to the conversation I want to have, "I want to go back to that card you sent me. The reason it disturbed me is, I am your sister and you wrote that you want me to think of you as my sister. What that meant to me was that you might want something different from me as your sister, something I am not. That hurts. I've always thought I was a good sister to you, just as you were a good brother to me. But I know that's changed, so I have to change everything I ever thought I knew. Suppose I could think of you as my sister. What do you imagine would change?"

"Not being one, I don't know what it's like to think like a girl. I guess if there were something where you would change the way you talk to me versus the way you talk to Texie, I'd like to know what that would be."

"Nothing would change, Gene. Anything I say to Texie I would say to you, and she would say the same thing about you talking to me. What went through my mind when I read your note was that you didn't want to talk about baseball anymore, or anything else we used to talk about, and I would miss that. I do miss that.

"And I have the feeling, especially when you keep saying 'girl,' that you want me to be a girl instead of a woman. The fact is, I don't know what girls think or say, because as I keep saying, I am not a girl. Perhaps you should talk to Lora (my eight-year-old granddaughter). She's a girl. She'd probably show you her barrettes and Barbies. Is that the kind of conversation you're looking for?"

Do I have to stoop to the sublime to reach him?

"I've always had a sense that it's easier to be a girl," he says, "and I'd like to know how that feels."

"Easier?"

"Yeah, like men have to be strong and make all the decisions and initiate things. We're supposed to lead, and it seems that women don't have to, even though they probably could."

"Gene! Damn it! You're still equating girls with men, not women with men. Girls do have it easier than men, because girls are children and men are grown-ups. Women are grown-ups just like men, and they don't have a damn thing easier than men. And as for what women could probably do, I could probably verbally rip your head off right now, but I won't because I don't want to ... even though I 'probably' could."

Gene just pauses and ignores me when I say ridiculous things like that. It's his version of tolerance. It's good that one of us is feeling tolerant.

"Other than your thinking that life would be easier," I continue sarcastically, "is there anything else that intrigues you about the possibility of experiencing life as a woman?"

"It seems to me that women come with a gift, even as girls. When I watch you operate, it seems like you're clued into something that we're not. And I don't know why I feel that way. It's just that when you're interacting among yourselves, it seems like there is something unspoken, maybe unconscious. Like you understand the world operates in a certain way and we don't. I don't know how to put that into words. I mean, I see it in Rachael ..."

"Like an intuition thing?"

"I guess."

"What is it you think we know something about?"

"I don't know. If I did know, you wouldn't be on that plane by yourselves. It just seems like ... I don't know if you've ever been around people who seem to be more clued in than you are, but that's how I feel when I'm around a bunch of women. I feel like I'm on a different planet."

"Well, you know, women are from Venus and men are from Mars ..."

"Yeah, yeah." He shoots me a 'get off that bull shit' look.

I deserve it. I don't care.

"I think I'm from Saturn, actually. You know, with all those protective rings around me. Which brings me back to your assumption that all girls, I mean women, are alike. Do you really believe that?"

"In that they're different from men? Yes."

"Men are different from other men. And women have differences from each other too. We're all individuals. You can't lump an entire sex into one big blob. I'd venture to guess that football players are different from mail clerks and machinists are different from court reporters. And they all probably have conversations that are similar sometimes and different sometimes."

"Girls sit around and talk about boys, I suppose, and about clothes," he responds.

It's obvious Gene has completely ignored everything I've said. He has his visions, and he's not going to let go of any of them. Back to girls, and back to what girls say and do. His entire life Gene has imagined what girls do, and right now he's consumed by what he's been imagining all those years. In his mind, we're all girls in women's clothing, just like Marilyn Monroe. Let me go find that pink satin dress I must have worn and let me try to retrieve my breathless, little-girl voice. NOT!

Gene needs to find out about girls either from real girls, or from women who cling to their childhood models. I don't know how to make that happen. He can't ask little girls these kinds of questions. Neither of us would force that scenario. And it wouldn't make sense to him anyway. In his mind, boys grow up and become macho, world-conscious men, and women don't grow up at all. They remain little girls, in their little pink dresses, dependent on men to protect and take care of them. It's an imagined dependency that Gene doesn't want to let go of. He wants the easy life of a woman who is a little girl. If these kinds of women exist, I don't know them.

I wouldn't call any woman I know and say, "I just bought fifty pairs of panties. Let's get together and talk about it."

If I made a call like that, we'd get together all right. She'd arrive at my place with the name of a shrink written on the back of her business card, which she'd hand to me and say, "Are you okay?"

Gene is lost in a world he imagined years ago; a world that didn't exist then, doesn't exist now, and will never represent today's real world. Do I bust his dream wide open, or try to support it? I don't think I can break it up. It's his fifty-year reality. It doesn't matter that it's not real. He's dreamed it for so long, it's real to him.

This is so frustrating. At first, my heart went out to him, and it still does. Having to live a lie is so demeaning. But the lie between us has passed, and the exposure hasn't brought us closer. He doesn't hear me anymore. He doesn't want to. He wants something else from me now. I'm yesterday's sister, and she's just not good enough.

"Maybe girls are boring," he says.

"Don't judge girls from my point of view."

I give up. If it's girls he wants, I'll give him his girl talk. It's better than screaming at him. Now I'm the one who lies. "What would you do if you were a girl?"

"If I were a girl, I could wear dresses and nail polish and makeup and stuff like that," he says. "We could have lunch and talk about it, and there would be no hassle."

"If you were a woman you might wear nail polish and makeup and stuff like that. If you were a girl, you would not." I couldn't hold my lie for even fifty seconds.

"Have we, man to woman, never talked about things like politics, world events, music and sports?" I roll on. "Aren't the Huskies and the Mariners fans about fifty percent female? Aren't there women's professional sports teams now—real ones with referees and uniforms and BALLS?"

"Fortunately," he says calmly in response to my raving, "in sports and some other areas, things are changing. But that's not what I'm looking for. I know how we're the same. I want to know more about how we're different. All I want is for you to not hold back on my account when you want to talk about girl stuff."

Aaargh!!! I don't talk about girl stuff. I'M NOT A GIRL!

You know what? Gene needs to know that when girls grow up and become women, we take our lingerie for granted. We're not putting on Mommy's jewelry, clothes and shoes, clomping around pretending to be ladies like our moms. We are the ladies; we are the moms. We don't have to pretend. We don't have to obsess about our undergarments. We know they're there ... under our garments. How do I get that across to him?

If Gene wants to join the world of women, he needs to better understand women. He needs to be with women besides me.

Or perhaps I'm the one who needs for him to meet other women. Do I need him to meet other women to validate my own womanhood? All of a sudden, I'm doubting my femininity. I'm experiencing the gut fear of prejudice. If I am among people who are different, I could become the one that's different. And that's damned uncomfortable.

SHIRLEYANNE THOM

Maybe I'll take another look at my lingerie drawers. They hold a lot more variety than I let on; not seventy-eight pairs of panties, but more than twenty. I'm going to touch them, to feel their softness. I need feminine validation from my lingerie drawer. Then I can share with Gene. And I'll review more of my feminine inclinations and find more things we can share.

Eeeew! No sharing of female "inclinations" with my bro. That's just not right. Can't do it. No way.

What ever are we going to do?

PART TWO

Chapter Fourteen

WEEKENDS HAVE CHANGED
I don't like my sister, or myself

It's another year and another Huskies football season. It's time to cheer our beloved Dawgs again. That's what we call 'em. Dawgs. Our Husky Dawgs. Two seasons ago, Gene and I sat in our Huskies football stadium as healthy siblings, cruising down our life roads together toward a happy and secure sunset.

Then one evening following a raucous, fan-filled home team victory, our private home team suddenly swerved onto another highway that took us away from all that we'd taken for granted. One evening changed our pasts, our present, and more than likely, our futures together. Will our future together be as separate as our past? Will we return to our comfortable secret lives? Or will we figure all this out? That's my hope. I hope we'll figure it out.

What each of us remembers about our past is different. He lived his secret life and I lived my blissfully ignorant life. I've at least got that figured out, and I've come to terms with it. What I can't figure is our future. Hell, I don't know how to figure today. So much has changed.

The first and most obvious change is Gene's health. I want to see some changes in his personal habits so I can be assured that he has taken his episode of congestive heart failure seriously. But I haven't witnessed any changes there. He still eats deep-fried chicken gizzards by the pound and he's grossly overweight.

"Gene, I worry about your health. You almost left this life a couple of years ago, and I'd like for my brother to stick around. That bag of deep-fried chicken gizzards you're eating is about as bad for your health as anything you could possibly eat."

"I'm not going to eat any fuckin' boring, bad-tasting food just to live a few extra months," were the exact words he threw back at me when I made this not-so-offhand remark about his eating deep-fried internal organs.

Obviously, I don't like his attitude, because his life definitely will be shortened if he doesn't change his diet. But I realize it's his choice and he is rightfully in charge of his own personal health. Never having married, and not having a mother around for over a decade, he's not going to respond to my nagging or casual remarks about his well-being. The issue of Gene's health is officially off the table, so to speak. His future on this earth will be as long as he wants it to be.

How that future is lived, as it relates to the two of us, is a shared responsibility, although Gene may not view the emotional responsibility as shared. In fact, he doesn't show any signs of thinking there is an emotional twist to any of this.

Now that he has come out to me, he can live his truth with no more hiding or pretending on his part. For the first time in our lives he can be his true self in my presence. He's more comfortable with our relationship now than he's ever been. He has someone to share his secret and he has a new place where he can dress up. A lifelong burden has been lifted from his florid shoulders.

Gene's been handed his personal pass to live his reality with me, and I truly don't begrudge him a single moment of his new-found freedom. But the fact is, the way he chooses to express his freedom has taken away my freedom when we're together. And we're together entirely too much.

Gene's coming out to me and the frequency of his visits to my home has put an emotional strain on my life. I have moved from being very comfortable with the two of us to being very uncomfortable with the two of us. His truth has not set me free. He's deliriously happy and I'm fuming. What's been lifted from my brother has been placed on me, and I have as much courage to deal with it as the dead chickens that have given him his favorite deep-fried snack.

Our weekends have changed dramatically. One change occurred through both necessity and choice. The necessity is due to his health. We don't walk up the stadium ramp to our seats. We take the chauffeured golf cart, like the rest of the old farts. This may seem to be a small change, and if it were isolated, it would be. A simple adjustment to accommodate a health issue should be a no-brainer. But because I'm making several adjustments, I'm cranky and less tolerant of each one.

Given my own robust health, I feel ridiculous taking up a seat on the handicap cart. It's hard for me to resist the urge to point to Gene as we pass people who are walking up the ramp, to let them know I'm riding along for the sole purpose of supporting the person beside me. It's not me, folks, with the handicap. It's my bro here. It's that guy. It's Him.

I don't like the way it feels to be different and dependent. In the process of coming to know more about my brother, I'm coming to know more about myself, and this particular bit of knowledge is disconcerting, to say the least.

I don't like being classified as handicapped or old. Does that mean I'm not as tolerant as I thought I was about other people's handicaps? A tiny little prejudice carefully tucked away is still a prejudice.

The truth is, I don't want to ride in a golf cart meant for incapacitated old geezers. I don't want to be one of them. Even more critical, I don't like how I'm feeling, knowing I'm feeling this way. This is a new look at myself, and I don't like what I see.

The other change is pure choice. Or at least I think it is pure choice. It has nothing to do with physical health or handicaps. This change comes after the game, when we return to my home. Gene still wears his brown cords and purple T-shirts to the game, but as soon as he walks into the condo he goes straight to his room and changes into a dress. He leaves the door open when he changes, which bugs the hell out of me.

I don't change with him. I could, but I don't want to. Putting on a silky dress to hang around home after a football game is not on my list of favorite postgame activities. It appears to be Gene's new favorite way to complete our Saturdays. There's nothing wrong with this new scenario. He does his thing and I do mine. Everything should be totally cool. But it's not.

I feel I should do more to support him. I feel I should change my clothes because I know he would like for me to change. It's Saturday night—party night—and women put on pretty dresses on party night. Well, crap. It's Saturday night in my own home and I'm second-guessing my choice of clothing. I'm thinking as much about clothes as he does. I'm becoming the dreaded frivolous. It's not as if he's asked me to dress up, but I seem to have acquired a new guilt trip that has usurped my ability to discern what's important and what's not. Amend that. I'm trying to make myself feel like I imagine how my brother feels. This is getting out of hand.

One thing I know for sure. Gene was right in his initial assessment as to how much we'd see of each other now that he can wear his real clothes around me. Even between football seasons, as witnessed this past year, I see much more of Gene than I used to, and definitely more of him than I want to, in more ways than I could ever have imagined. Accommodating his presence and all it entails has become a burr under the familiar saddle of my contented lifestyle.

So, you want to wear a dress, Gene? No problem. Whatever you wear is perfectly okay with me, so GET THE FUCK OVER IT! Put on your damn dress and let's get back to your playing the banjo while I sew or read or paint. Where the hell is your banjo, anyway?

Let's talk politics. How about those damned Republicans and their stupid "Contract with America?" Newt's a phony. Anyone with a real brain knows that. How'd he get to be front page news? And what the hell is Clinton doing screwing an ugly intern? These are important news items that require our attention. The world's a mess and we need to fix it. Do you remember how we used to solve the world's problems in one sitting? Pinky cannot rule the world without The Brain.

Hanging with Gene used to be a great way to spend a weekend. First of all, it was limited to six times a year for Huskies football, and a few more weekends for Seattle Mariners baseball. I knew when he'd arrive, and I knew when he'd leave. I have no problem fixing weekend meals six-to-twelve times a year. It was dinner Saturday night and breakfast Sunday morning, with ball games and scintillating conversations filling the hours in between. Perfect.

Second, not all hours of the weekend were filled with just the two of us. Gene would go to the Aviator Store and pick up periodicals with the latest news of the airline industry. He keeps a catalog of all the airliners Boeing has ever built. It's an amazing collection of facts, spanning decades of flight.

In addition, Gene would go to a bluegrass jam every once in a while, at someone else's house. Sometimes I'd tag along. We both love those old-timey tunes. Occasionally, we'd eat out or take in a live musical performance at the Tractor Tavern. I didn't feel responsible for making sure Gene had a satisfying weekend every minute of every weekend. He seemed to want to do things on his own. That left me with time to be alone to do my own things. Those kinds of weekends left me relaxed and ready to hit the media sales madness for another week. That's just not so, anymore. After our weekends together, I'm emotionally drained when Monday finally arrives.

In addition to the frequency of his presence, the nature of his presence is a strain. And it's not the obvious change in his outer apparel; it's the change in what should be the less-obvious apparel. Gene is so proud of his clothes, all his clothes, that he has to show them all off, all the time. We're talking about underwear here. He hangs around the condo in his undies. Let me tell you, a five-foot-ten, 260-pound, fifty-six year-old male walking around the house in his bra, panties, and slip is not a pleasant sight. I can truthfully say it's not the kind of underwear he wears that bothers me.

Whether he struts around the house in pink silk panties or blue cotton boxer shorts is not the issue. I've never hung out with my brother in his underwear, or anyone else for that matter. Texie and Jaqi and I don't hang out in our underwear, and my daughters and I don't hang out in our underwear. I don't even hang out by myself in my underwear. And I don't care to start doing so now. Gene, for God's sake, get dressed!

This new "exposure" on his part has cultivated a goofy kind of paranoia that has me wanting to make sure I'm covered from chin to toes every moment of the day, as if to demonstrate that being covered up is the preferred dress code around here. Rather than amble into the kitchen to put on a pot of coffee when I first get up, I sneak to the front door, grab the newspaper, and scurry back to my bed to read, because I don't want to venture into the living room in anything less than a full covering of clothes.

Furthermore, one does not get into full dress mode without showering, washing one's hair, applying deodorant, and brushing one's teeth. By the time I emerge from my self-imposed bedroom cocoon, it's almost high noon, and I'm ready to march down the middle of Main Street in Tombstone with my Colt .45 loaded, ready to drop my brother in his delicate little tracks. I am so frustrated!

When I finally do venture into the living room, in casual attire appropriate for a Sunday at home, I am met either with an under-clad goofball or a vision of silk and pearls, waiting for me to comment on his latest outfit. I don't give a rat's ass what he's waiting for. I'm not going to comment. I am so pissed off at being a prisoner in my own home that if I say anything at all, I'll blow the roof off this place. And then he'll go away and I'll feel like the biggest jackass on the face of the earth, and he'll think my agitation means I really do care that he's weird.

No. Let me amend that. My brother is not weird. He's a perfectly normal heterosexual cross-dresser who's forcing me to deal with his proud new identity—always! It's the always that is begging for relief.

Did I say perfectly normal cross-dresser? There is no such thing as normal, and even if there were such a thing, I don't know or care what it is. All I know is, I want to return to having a well-rounded, thoughtful, not-in-my-personal space brother who is easy and fun to hang out with. I don't want to spend my weekends with an obsessed, single-minded frou-frou. I don't pick silly girl-friends, and I don't like having a silly brother who wants to be my sister, fer Chrissake! I want my good ol' bro back.

It's not Gene's fault my head is so full of turmoil. He has no idea this fool-ishness is roiling around inside my head. He assumes everything is all right, and why shouldn't he? I'm prancing around lah-dee-dah-ing as if everything is so-oo cool. I'm Ms. Wonderful, full of acceptance, the epitome of tolerance for all that is good or bad or anywhere in between. Go ahead, Gene, be yourself and do whatever you want. Just don't do it around me, unless I have complete control over when and where and how you do it. Tolerant, my ass. I'm the most intoler-ant person I've ever known. All the worse because I pretend to be something I'm not.

Whew! That was a torrent of self-flagellation. Feel better now? You know, most of this could be fixed with a simple thing known as conversation. Have yourself a sit down with your brother, ST. Set some guidelines. Tell him you can't go from brown cords to silk panties in one fell swoop—not because you prefer cords to panties, but because cords are outerwear and panties are underwear. I don't mind seeing my brother in outerwear, even if it's a dress. I do mind seeing my brother in underwear. It's called underwear for a reason. It's meant to be under the outer ... under. Have I beat this dog to death yet? UNDER wear.

A year and a half ago, Gene said to me, "This is who I am." Well, Gene, this is who I am. I'll listen to who you are, and I'll try to understand, but if I don't, that doesn't mean I am rejecting you. It only means I don't understand. I am a private person, and these attempts at exposure are draining me. And damn it! I shouldn't have to change who I am to Gene because Gene has changed who he is to me.

I am not frivolous. I am not your impression of who girls are. Allow me to be the strong, bold, and tolerant person I imagine myself to be. I'll work harder on the tolerance, if you'll allow me to keep my feminine side where I've chosen to put it, close to myself and close to those persons I wish to expose it to, mean-ing those people who like me the way I am.

Once upon a time I may have been as sweet and soft and feminine as you would like a sister to be. But I don't remember such a time. It would have been before I worked my ass off to raise two kids on my own, blah, blah, blah. They turned out to be mighty fine grown-ups. And the person I am today is the person who got us here, and this is the person that will keep me here. I can't go back. And even if I could go back, I don't happen to want to go back.

I prefer that you not walk around my home in your underwear, Gene. I won't be showing you my intimate wear and I'm not interested in you showing me yours. I put clean underwear on my body every morning and put my not-too-clean underwear in the hamper every night. That's all the time I care to devote to the wearing of underwear. I don't want to spend weekends with you observing and discussing intimate apparel. And it would be the same even if we were sisters. You have a warped sense of how women behave, and you don't want to accept the truth as to how we do behave. You want to believe your false fantasies. So, believe them. But they are false, and I don't want to spend so many of my weekends supporting them anymore.

I miss the weekends we used to have. I also miss the weekends we didn't have; the weekends I used to share with other people, like my grandkids, and the weekends I had to myself. I still want to see you, but not so much. I need to give this a rest.

This thing is so in-your-face, so omnipresent. I am beginning to empathize with Mom. I've only dealt with this for two years. She dealt with it for many years, not knowing when it would pop up in her face again. Maybe she needed a rest too.

Who the Hell cares? I'm sick of Gene, and I'm sick of myself too. In fact, I'm sick of the whole damn thing. Maybe I'll just go throw up in my less-than-pointy-toed shoes and be done with it.

Oh Gawd! I'm ranting again. If I happen to find the courage to say these things out loud to Gene, he'll patiently wait for me to stop, flash me his trademark indulgent smile, and carry on as if nothing had been said. He'll continue to ignore my needs as he panders to his.

No smiling at me, Gene. It ain't funny.

Is too.

Is not.

Chapter Fifteen

GENE'S HAD ENOUGH OF ME
My little problem is solved

Another year has passed. It's been more than three years now since my brother greeted me at my condo door wearing his flowered dress and fishnet hose. Being confronted with his "out" was a bit unsettling at first. But I was more concerned with the secrecy of it than the actual sight of it. I wondered, "Why now?" rather than, "What now?"

I recall being more than a little pissed off that this big secret occurred and endured throughout our family history, and I'm still pissed about that. I always will be. In fact, I thought the family secret thing would be the hardest part of this new-found knowledge for me to overcome. But I have to admit, it has given me a useful tool to explain my arm's length approach to emotional survival.

This big family secret is serving as my excuse for being a loner. I now have something I can point to as the reason for my aloofness, for this great ability I've developed to separate myself at a certain point in a relationship and walk away to the safe zone of noncommitment. It's what makes me the "so strong I can handle anything" person that I profess to be. It has become very useful. I don't have to speak to my brother. I don't have to tell him I don't like him anymore. I can keep up the façade and keep everyone and everything ignorantly humming along.

But another year has passed and no one is humming. I know it's not the family secret thing. There is no secret anymore. It started out so easy, with two gals shopping. I think I said to myself at the time that it was going to be a cinch. I had just bought my brother a dress, and it was so easy. And that was so foolish. It was not easy.

Another year has passed and Gene and I are estranged.

I thought my brother would be wearing dresses more than pants when I first saw him in his flowery dress, and that was just fine with me. What I didn't comprehend in those first moments was that his wearing dresses would be just a small part of what would change. I didn't know that wearing dresses and bras and panties and slips and stockings and pearls and purses, and whatever the hell else we women put on our bodies, would become an obsession for him that I would be sick of seeing and hearing about.

I didn't think my brother would be expecting so much from me. I wish he was still my same ol' brother, but he's not. I'm sure Gene is a happier person now, and for that I am truly pleased for him. But I am not a happier person. I have lost my favorite lifelong companion. My brother is gone from me, and not just metaphorically. Gene is really gone. I don't know if or when I will see him again.

He left me a few weeks ago. It was a Sunday morning. He knocked on my bedroom door and told me he was leaving and he wouldn't be back. He said I've changed. I didn't want to lose him; I told him I didn't want him to go. I told him I hadn't changed; that it really was okay for him to stay. But it was noon, and I was still hiding in my bedroom. And he left me there.

Now I'm pissed off again. He has the gall to sit in my living room, month after month, wearing his goddamn dresses, and watching that goddamn television screen ten hours a day, when he's not snoring, that is; leaving me bereft of any kind of in-depth conversations we used to have; leaving me no time for friends and grandkids—and he tells me I've changed. I have not changed. He's the one who changed. To Hell with him.

He won't be coming down from Bellingham for a while, to go to the Washington Huskies' football games with me. He won't be coming down from Bellingham for a while, to go to the Seattle Mariners' baseball games with me. The Huskies are 6 and 1 for the season so far, and the Mariners almost made the playoffs, and I've been going to the games without my brother. The two of us have been going to baseball games together for more than forty years. I am still going to baseball games, but we aren't going with each other, because he says I've changed.

Our country will have a new president in a few weeks and we haven't sat down and cussed out the Republicans yet. Violence has broken out in the Middle East again, and Boeing is losing sales to Europe's Airbus, and Gene and I haven't discussed why these things are happening, or offered up our grand solutions for correcting these misdeeds and business decisions.

Ken Griffey, Jr. left the Mariners last year, and Alex Rodriguez is a free agent. We're losing our best players and Gene and I haven't figured out yet how we're going to field a competitive major league baseball team without them.

What's going to happen to everything and everybody? I don't know. Gene and I aren't talking. We haven't had these kinds of discussions in a long, long time. He wants girl talk and I don't do his version of girl talk. I never have. But he says I've changed.

Today is October 21. Today is Gene's birthday. Two weeks ago, I had a birthday. Four years ago, on my birthday, Gene nearly died. I stood in my living room and watched what I believed to be a futile effort by six paramedics to save his life. He was a purplish-dark gray color and not breathing on his own. He physically survived the trauma of that night, but the brother I knew did not survive. He began to leave me four years ago, on that very night. We've never made a big deal of our birthdays, but somehow we managed to acknowledge them with cards, family gatherings, and whatever. No word from Gene on my birthday, and no word from me to Gene on his.

You have to call Gene at work between nine and noon on Friday. He chooses not to have a phone at home, so I've always called him at work and sung "Happy Birthday to you …" to him. It's silly. But most traditions are. Today was Friday. I got busy and just plain forgot to call him, until it was too late to reach him. I forgot my brother on his birthday. Perhaps I *have* changed.

How have we come to this? In a word, we were naïve. Gene's coming out was too easy. Because I didn't, and still don't, care what he wears. I thought the unveiling of a cross-dresser, after the initial uncomfortable moments, would be no big deal. But Gene has a compelling need to feel feminine fabrics against his skin. That doesn't bother me. While I knew that it would bother most people, I have never been beholden to the crush of societal mores. He could bring his dresses and lingerie when he came to visit me, and put on whatever he wanted to wear at my place. It was all right with me. I thought that was all it would be about. No big deal, as far as I could tell.

Obviously, it proved to be much, much more. Wearing dresses is a very big deal to Gene, and he wanted it to be a big deal to me too. After being closeted for most of his life, Gene needs for it to be a big deal. My big shrug at first was a relief to him, and it gave him a measure of comfort to be able to acknowledge his real self. Over time, however, my casual acceptance about the whole disclosure became a disappointment to him. He expected more from his outing than I gave him. He expected me to become his version of what he dreamed his sister would be, once she knew she had a sister.

Gene wanted me to care about what he wears. He wanted to talk about hair and clothes and nail polish, and he wanted us to share secret passions, like he imagined sisters do. And maybe some sisters do all that. I never had a sister, so I wouldn't know.

I expected Gene to remain the same brother who now happens to wear dresses in my presence. I expected our time together would be about the same. He'd come down for a game on Saturday and we'd have dinner together. Sometimes we'd hang together after dinner and sometimes he'd go play music with his friends. Sunday after breakfast he'd go to the Aviator Store on his way back home.

One wonderful part of his being my brother was that I felt no obligation to treat him as a guest. Our time together was a relaxing hang time with someone I cared about and whose company I enjoyed. The other wonderful part, I now know, was that it was time-bound and fit nonintrusively into my very tightly packed life. He was my friendly oasis from the pack.

I have obligations, obligations that I enjoy, but obligations nevertheless. My work is stressful and takes between fifty and sixty hours of my time each week. It's media, and it's competitive, and it's social. People, people, people all day, all the time.

I also have two little families that are made up of two lovely daughters, two great sons-in-law, and five beautiful grandchildren ranging in age from six months to thirteen years. We share as much as we can.

I have friends and season tickets to the opera and a membership in the Seattle Art Museum. I also like to read and write and paint, by myself. Time to myself is scarce and very precious. I had time to myself when I was growing up and I got used to having it.

I grew up in a family of four people who were emotionally reserved by nature. I never learned to share secrets and passions with other people. The closest I ever came to feeling I had a confidante was in my relationship with my brother, Gene. Now that's gone. I drove him away.

I had longed to return to the safety of the silent, voiceless communication system I developed and perfected over the years. It was my version of returning to the nest.

I got what I thought I wanted. Do I feel better now?

Chapter Sixteen

I FINALLY GET OVER MYSELF
And quit wallowing in the past

Last night I went to bed an angry, whining idealist trying to find ways to excuse my insistent existence. This morning I awaken a realist … not a defeated realist, but rather an enlightened and humbled realist, who has left her raging ego somewhere between the bed sheets and her pillow.

My anger was directed toward the two people I've been writing about. How could my mother and my brother have lied to themselves and to me for more than forty years? I said to myself. How could they do that to themselves and to me? How dare they not be my heroes? How dare they disappoint me?

I'll tell you how they dared. They dared so they could live their lives to completion. They dared to be ordinary people trying to survive by coping as best they could with their human frailties. I wanted them to be brave pioneers, blazing trails of independent thought and decisive action. Their frailty disappointed me, and I was angered by my disappointment. They could have told me everything, I reasoned, and my support would have set them free.

Mom could have spilled her guts to me and told me she was a scared young woman, walking a tightrope of bravado as she did her very best to provide a decent living for herself and her family. I could have hugged her and said it was okay that she was scared. I could have assured her that her fear didn't matter; that confiding in me would have made everything all better. I could have told her that, of course, but that would have been a vast acre of bull shit. What did I know about basic survival?

I wasn't born poor and I didn't have to leave home at age thirteen to find my own identity. I didn't have to pull my family out of a pig farm on the outskirts of a boomtown during a World War, and dash my husband's investment dreams. And I didn't have to protect a child who happened to be of another stream of life; the kind of stream that would have ridiculed him into an early pit of shame. Mom coped with all those things and I did not. How dare I be disappointed in her!

Gene could have told me of his cross-dressing tendencies and walked beside my brave front, and he would have been shielded by my bravery. That, too, is a field of crap. How brave would it have been for me to offer empathy during my all-too-gallant moments of standby support while he dealt with daily attacks against instinctive feelings that somehow didn't fit in with society's perceived notions of what is, or should be, normal behavior? How much courage does it take for me, with my six-figure salary, to tell him to dress any way he wants to dress, while he fears being sacked from his own employment for expressing himself openly? He said he didn't want to tell me because he thought I would be disappointed in him. He was right to withhold his secret from me. How dare I be disappointed in him?

I woke up this morning with nothing but awe for these two people who have dealt with far more diversity and hardship than I will ever experience.

It's time for me to fix this relationship with my brother. Hopefully, I'm not too late.

Chapter Seventeen

MOM RETURNS
In a dream

I'm standing next to Gene's hospital bed. He's lying there on top of the covers, very still. His eyes are closed. I've been here for what seems like days, and I'm exhausted. Nothing has changed for several hours. I think it's safe to take a break.

"Bye, Gene, I'll be back soon," I say as I prepare to leave the room to get a bite to eat. Approaching the door, I feel something change. It's that "strange presence" thing again. Now what? I turn around and look back toward Gene.

Damn! What is she doing there?!? She's been gone so long. Why has she come back? It can't be for any good reason. Oh no… NO! I race from the door back to Gene's bed and throw myself on top of him, sobbing. With tearful eyes I raise my head and turn to her.

"Get out of here!" I shout. "You're not wanted here … GO … NOW!"

Our mother turns her head away from Gene and looks at me passively. She's not interested in my hysterics. She doesn't care about me. It's Gene she wants. She's here to get Gene. He appears oblivious, lying there with his eyes closed. I don't think she's reached him yet. I may still have time to save him.

I pull myself off of Gene and muscle my way into the chair she occupies, forcing her to stand. I'm taking over this gig. The one thing ghosts cannot do is fight back, if a live person shows no fear, and she's not going to get the satisfaction of seeing my fear. She glares at me, waiting for me to bow my head or slump my shoulders or emit any of those obvious signs of dreaded resolve. Well, Mom, I don't slump, and you don't scare me, so GET THE HELL OUT OF THIS ROOM!

Poof! She's gone. Ha! I'm in the chair now, back in control. I won't be taking any more breaks. I have to be here to keep the ghosts away until I know Gene is safe. I stand up to take his hand and assure him that I won't leave him alone again. She can't come back as long as I'm here. I'll stand guard. He doesn't have to go anywhere he doesn't want to go.

But I can't take his hand.

There's another hand approaching my brother and it's zipping up the black sheet Gene's lying on. It wasn't black a few minutes ago. The white bed sheet has turned black and it's morphing into a plastic body bag, closing around him. The hand pulls the zipper up, up, up. I stand beside Gene, frozen, as I watch him disappear inside the bag. The zipper is near his face now. His face disappears inside the black bag. His blond curls are the last part of him that I see.

Chapter Eighteen

WE'RE BACK TOGETHER
Gene faces surgery

My eyes fly open. I'm lying here in my own bed, in my own bedroom. There is no hospital bed. It's my own bed, and I'm in it. But there's also no relief. I've had another of my dreaded death dreams. I saw Dad in a casket six months before he was diagnosed with lung cancer. Years later I dreamed I was on a boat carrying a baby across the River Styx. The baby was my mother. Six weeks after my dream, she was diagnosed with lung cancer. Now, years after she died, she has appeared in a dream to take Gene away to her side of the river. Gene is next up. Oh shit, oh dear.

It's a Seattle Mariners' weekend and Gene is reading the Sunday paper in my living room. I can hear the pages rustling. ESPN Sunday morning is on TV. They're showing last night's baseball scores. I hear Gene shift channels to the Indy 500. The gentlemen have started their engines, and Gene is watching the race sitting on the couch in my living room, wearing a new bright green dress.

A year ago, I would have been pissed out of my mind for no good reason and stayed in my bedroom, using the dream as my excuse for dallying. But as they say, that was then; this is now.

We're together again because we have a wonderful extended family and because of that fabulous game of baseball. Our reconciliation came about quite naturally. We are part of a core group of eighteen extended family members who get together for every major holiday, and for every birthday of a child in our newest generation. I certainly wasn't going to give up our family get-togethers, and neither was Gene. The family gatherings have allowed us to take a time out from each other and return to our individual comfort zones; back to pleasantries, at neutral sites.

Then I heard the Seattle Mariners were offering a new season-ticket week-end package. Seats were available in right field, right behind Ichiro, and it cost only $800 to go to every Friday, Saturday and Sunday home game. Such a deal!

I called Gene at work and asked him if he would be interested in going in with me on a couple of seats.

"Yeah," he said. What a wonderful word.

"Yeah."

We did have a little sit-down the Saturday morning of his first weekend back. This time I was determined to get it right. No more playing martyr. The problem of weekend expectations simply had to be settled. I couldn't return to giving entire weekends over to what I believed were his self-centered desires.

"Gene," I said, "I don't want to spend every weekend taking pictures of you in all your outfits. And I don't want to wake up every Sunday morning feeling I have to comment on what you're wearing. You can wear whatever you want, but I don't want to feel obligated to make your attire the singular subject of our weekend conversations."

He looked up at me and I diverted my eyes, not knowing if he was going to get up and leave immediately, or stick it out this weekend and not return ever again.

He paused and said in a reverent voice, "I hereby absolve you from taking pictures of me all weekend, and from commenting on my Sunday attire."

Whew! I'm so glad we finally had that talk … our sixty-second family version of "that talk". Who says it has to take hours, or days, or years to solve life's crises?

In a few hours we'll walk to Safeco Field and watch the Seattle Mariners play the Baltimore Orioles. Last year, the M's won 116 games, tying the 1906 Cubbies for most wins in a single season. This year is looking pretty good too. But right now, I think I'll mosey into the living room and sit on the other end of the sofa and watch the cars roar around the oval track. It's Memorial Day weekend and it's Indy Race time. And I'll read the paper with my bro. And I'll forget I had that dreadful dream. I begin to work the crossword puzzles.

"Gene, what's JFK's mother's name … four letters?"

"Rose."

I knew that. My mother is interfering with my concentration. What the hell was she doing in my bedroom, messing with my head? Selfish, self-centered bi---. She had plenty of time to take care of her son and help him feel good about himself. Why do you want him now, Mom? Do you want to make sure his afterlife is a miserable place too? Oooo, Gene wouldn't like these thoughts. I thought I'd made peace with her during my overnight enlightenment a few months back, but here she is again and she's up to her same old control games.

After an hour or so, I get up to take a shower and get ready for the game. Dressed in my Mariner Blues, I re-enter the living room and see Gene still on the sofa, watching television in his green dress.

"I have this overwhelming urge to wear a dress all day today," he says. "I'm not going to the game."

Hmm. He seldom misses a game. Something's up.

The phone rings. It's Cousin Texie, and she's crying. "Dad's on his way to Yakima in an ambulance. He's had a stroke and …."

"I'm coming over. We'll go together."

"I'll go crazy waiting for you to get here."

"Then you come here and pick me up. You are not driving 150 miles by yourself to get there."

"Oh, okay," she says. I hang up, and tell Gene what's happening.

"Have you had one of your dreams lately?" he asks. And he thinks it's only women who are clued in. I didn't even hint that I'd had a dream. How do I answer this?

"Yes," I respond. "I had one this morning as a matter of fact, just before I woke up. That's why I've been quiet."

I don't like to talk about my spooky dreams. I told Gene about the Mom and Dad dreams, but those were years and years ago. Why is he asking me this question now? I never ever tell the person who is the subject of a dream. What'll I say? He's waiting for me to elaborate.

"It wasn't about Dick," I say.

He continues to look at me, expectantly. It might be the right time to tell him about my trip to the doctor last week. That'll satisfy him.

"I guess I should tell you that I had a body scan last Tuesday. It revealed a bunch of lesions inside me. My doctor doesn't know what they are yet, but he says they're probably nothing. In fact, doctors don't like it when people have those scans, because most people have cysts and lesions inside their bodies that mean nothing and they get all excited about nothing. I only did it because Dad and Mom died so young and because tendencies toward cancer sometimes are genetic. I wanted to get a base-line read on my health. One of the lesions is on my pancreas. They want to take a closer look at that. Pancreases aren't supposed to have lesions, or whatever they call it. It could be trouble. The dream could have been a result of my medical probing."

Boy! I dropped a load of information—information I'd been avoiding dealing with myself. I haven't told anybody else yet. Nervous chatter? Maybe the dream was about me. No. Mom clearly came to get Gene, not me.

"I had tests last Tuesday, too," he says. "We already took a closer look. I have prostate cancer."

"Okay, you're sicker than I am. You win."

We look at each other and laugh. We laugh like we haven't laughed in a long, long time. In one moment of terrible news we realize that nothing of real consequence has come between us. Our laughter is a release. The long months of tension are erased. Gene has cancer. Nothing else really matters, does it? Is he my brother or my sister? Who the Hell cares!

I feel a chill run down my spine and a stab of pain hit my heart. We've come so far, and now we won't have time to enjoy our new chapter. It's not fair!

"Remember last fall when I lost my job at AT&T?" I ask. "You asked me if I could afford to retire, and I said, 'If I don't live very long.' You said that applied to you too. Well, it looks like we might be able to retire."

It's my feeble attempt at humor.

"Actually, I'm kind of relieved about me," he says. "My retirement account isn't looking very good right now. The Republicans have taken care of that."

"Damn Republicans."

Now we're really talking like we used to.

Neither of us has lived a prudent life. Gene likes expensive sports cars and sports tickets; I like expensive travel, and art, and sports tickets. We can't afford those things if we live a long life. He could sell one of his two MR2's, and I suppose I could part with one of my Miró aquatints, or my new Marc Chagall lithograph, or the Picasso etching hanging over the toilet in my private bath. But that's not how we think. I'd rather have the company of Mr. Chagall today than survive ninety years of being aesthetically deprived.

"What are your options?" I ask.

"My doctor has given me information to help me decide. I can have radiation bullets, or chemotherapy, or surgery. They're always afraid to tell a man he's going to lose his prostate gland," he says with a sly grin, "but virility is not on my list of treasured attributes. I'll probably go for the surgery."

"How long do you have to decide?"

"A couple of weeks."

Texie arrives and we leave Gene behind as we head for a weekend in a Yakima hospital waiting room. I'm not worried about Uncle Dick. He's safe for now. I can't tell Texie this, of course, because it's not appropriate to talk about Gene and me when our primary concern today is Uncle Dick. Today's energy must be directed toward sending positive vibes to her dad.

When we arrive at the hospital, we get a call from Gene. He's decided to come to Yakima to be with us.

Because it's a holiday weekend, we have an extra day off. Monday morning, we get the report on Uncle Dick's tests and, sure enough, he's going to be all right. It wasn't a stroke. A blood clot landed on the outside of his brain, not inside his brain; it'll be treatable with medication. Texie wants to stay here with her family a bit longer. I ride back to Seattle with Gene.

"So, have you decided what you're going to do?" I ask. I know he said a couple of weeks, but we've had a couple of days of family mortality surrounding us. Maybe he's made some decisions.

"It seems to me that surgery is the only way we'll know for sure if it's localized or if it's spread, so I'm leaning toward surgery."

"At least you have options. It's when they say the word 'inoperable' we know we're in deep doo-doo. It's been a long time, but we've heard that word before."

"Yeah."

Okay, it looks like I'll have to dig the details out of him. What a surprise.

"Will the surgery be in Bellingham?"

"Yeah."

"How many days will you be in the hospital?"

"Three to five. When I leave, I'll have to have a catheter for a couple of weeks, then diapers for a few months. I may be incontinent."

"Bummer."

It's quiet in the car for about fifty miles of road.

Gene breaks the silence first. "I'll stay with you, if that's ok."

This is not unexpected so it's not complete panic that runs through me, but my stress level has definitely soared. Gene gets the den when he stays for the weekend and that works for a weekend. I'm now self-employed and my office is the den. I don't know how I'll manage my work, if he's with me during the week. But it's not like there are options as to where he will recuperate. It'll be my place and I'll figure it out.

"Sure. How long?"

"I've applied for six weeks' leave time at work."

Six weeks? Holy crap! That indicates serious convalescence. I'm not a nurse. His disease is very personal. Does he expect me to change his catheter? That's not going to happen. I'll hire a nurse. But what about my office? How's that going to work?

"When?" I ask.

"I've checked the Mariners' schedule. They're out of town for a stretch in July. I'm thinking July 8."

"That's quite a ways away." Heaven forbid that cancer surgery should cause us to miss a Mariners game.

"Prostate cancer is slow-growing."

At least he's determined a course of action. All I know in my situation is I've got a bunch of 'it could be nothing' lesions. 'It could be nothings' coming from doctors usually mean it could be something, but we don't know what yet. I turn up the bluegrass music.

The following week, a closer look-see reveals about as much information as the first scan I had, but some things can be ruled out. The lesions appear to be benign, not-to-worry cysts, except for the one on or near the head of my pancreas. Dr. Smith wants a specialist to look at it to eliminate serious concern. The specialist is Dr. Schueffler. He's a gastroenterologist. I've seen him before for acid reflux. He's booked until July 12, four days after Gene's surgery. Because it's difficult to get in to see Dr. Schueffler, I take the appointment. The week of July 8 could make for some interesting times.

The next few weeks bring on a tidal wave of emotions—from deep concern about Gene's cancer to equal concern about his surviving the surgery. I'm as worried about the surgery as I am about the results of it. He's managed to come up with onset diabetes, due to his obesity. Neither the cause nor the result of his obesity makes for simple surgeries. I silently curse him for his cavalier attitude regarding his overall health. And there is that little detail as to what my tests will dump on us. Will I be available to harbor him?

"Gene, has the doctor asked you to do anything special to prepare for surgery?" (Like go on a DIET?!?)

"I've got a bunch of forms to fill out, and they want me to name a power of attorney for medical decisions. I figured it would be you."

"Yeah, I'll do it." How about health directives; how about a will?

"I'll give you all the information about the surgery and recovery. I'll have to have a catheter for a few weeks, and I'll probably have to wear a diaper for at least six months."

Oh Lord. He had to say that again. Once was enough. I am not going to deal with catheters and things of that sort for my brother. I am not a healthcare professional. And I have no idea how I'm going to manage weeks of facing pee sacks and a brother in a short nightie while I try to live and run a business in my small condo. What on God's earth am I going to do? Gene doesn't want anyone to know about this until it's almost surgery time. I respect his wishes, but I am going to have to get counsel from someone. I don't know who to talk to.

• • • • •

Texie and I take a long-planned short vacation the last week of June to San Francisco to see *Tosca* in the Opera House, and to roam around the Bay area for a few days. The first night there we do a bit of bar hopping. At one stop, over my old friend Jack Rocks, I spill the new family news.

"I have some bad news."

Great way to start a vacation. Out it comes in one big rush. "Gene has prostate cancer. He's chosen to have surgery. It's scheduled for a week from Monday in Bellingham. He's going to do his recovery at my place. He didn't want me to tell anyone yet, but ... I don't know what the heck I'm going to do. He expects me to take care of him."

"How can he expect you to do that? That's not going to work," she says.

I ignore that. "I am very uncomfortable with his recovering ninety miles away from his doctor, especially the first week."

"Well, you can't take care of him yourself. That's asking too much."

"If he needs daily medical attention, I'll hire a nurse. And I've thought through the space arrangements. I'll turn over the master suite to him, so he'll have the privacy of bed and bath to himself. The bed in the den is comfortable. I've slept on it before."

"How long?"

"He's taking six weeks."

"I don't think I could do that."

"Yes, you could."

Time passes quickly. We're back in Seattle and a dreaded activity has approached. I've asked Texie to prepare the necessary legal papers to prepare for medical decision-making and final allocations—'final' meaning Last Will and Testament. And I've asked our friends Cliff and Mary to be the signatory witnesses to all the legalese.

We might as well make it a party. Gene's surgery is set for next Monday, so I've invited Cliff and Mary and Texie to join us for dinner Sunday night at my place, to get all the legal work done and send Gene to the hospital in style. We'll all dress up in party clothes.

I prepare roast chicken, a favorite meal of Gene's, with biscuits, and potatoes and gravy, and boysenberry pie à la mode for dessert. It's a last supper I hope won't be a last supper. But there's one tiny glitch to the feast. Gene can't eat any of it. He's on surgery alert. Oops! I forgot that little detail. All he gets to have is one final drink of that pinkish white chalky crap that empties his bowels.

Another kind of crap is flying at me for forgetting that wee detail. Gene sits at the table watching us eat roast chicken while he sips the chalky stuff.

"Mmm, good," he says about every three minutes.

"Want some pie, Gene? Berry's your favorite, next to lemon meringue," I throw back at him. "I fixed it just for you."

"Is it any better than the lemon pies that tasted like piss you used to try to poison me with?"

"Okay, so I'm not a world-class pie maker. I have other attributes."

"Like what?"

"Like putting up with your brand of shit."

After dinner it's music, just like old times. We stay away from the familiar themes of train wrecks and death-by-heartbreak tunes so core to bluegrass and old-timey ditties. It's more like the "Keep on the Sunny Side of Life" songs.

I take pictures of Gene in his maroon print dress balancing a banjo on his knee. "Oh, he came from Alabama with a banjo on his silky-flower-printed skirt …."

I think of Mom, who loved this kind of evening, and I mentally warn her to stay the Hell away from us. Later, as Gene signs the final papers turning everything he owns over to me, he issues his own warning: "My red car better be here when I get out."

In the kitchen, Texie asks me if I've decided what I'm going to do. Of course, I have. It's a no-brainer. I'm very worried about the surgery, and that concern has put a bottom line to all of my so-called choices.

"Tomorrow, I'm driving my brother to the hospital for cancer surgery. When it's over, I'd rather drive him back here than not drive him anywhere again. It's a pretty simple decision."

It's been a wonderful evening with family and friends, not unlike many such occasions we've shared throughout our years together. I don't know what tomorrow will bring, but I do know I don't want life with Gene to be over. Out … Damn Dream!

Gene is wearing a dress to the hospital. If it's to be his last outing, he says, he's going out as his real self, not as an imposter in brown cords. I decide to go along with the dress-up factor. No pants for me either. No one at the hospital says a word about our attire. They give him the usual lovely shapeless, petit-print cotton hospital gown to change into and we sit down to wait for the anesthesiologist to come and begin the prep.

Last Friday, I told a Latino friend about my dream. Frankly, I'm scared. My friend says, according to his ethnic lore, I must tell Gene about it, because to tell it will make the threat go away.

"Gene has to know of his peril so he can face it down," he says.

"So, Gene, if you happen to see a spook in the O. R., tell her to take a hike," I say.

He looks at me quizzically, indicating he thinks I'm losing my mind again. I love that look.

I continue. "On Memorial Day, before you told me about the cancer, you asked me if I'd had any dreams lately. I told you, yes, but I didn't tell you the dream was about you. I dreamed that you were in the hospital and Mom had parked herself next to your bed, waiting to take you with her to whatever plane she's sitting on. I chased her away, but I feel her lurking. If you see her, tell her to take a flying fu …"

He gives me his sly grin as the doctors approach us. I watch them wheel him down the hall to who knows what fate. He gives me the same grin when he opens his eyes in the recovery room six hours later. It looks like he faced her down, and he won.

Hot damn! He does look good!

Mom is gone, and my brother is here. We're moving on!

Chapter Nineteen

MY TURN
A lucky dress will protect me

"Let's put her back under and take another look."

That's what I hear as I'm coming out of the effects of a general anesthetic. Put me back under? What the Hell …

A couple of hours later I wake up in a multibed recovery room at the University of Washington Medical Center. I've been sent here for a special kind of arthroscopic look at that not-to-worry-about lesion on my pancreas. This procedure allows the doctors to take a biopsy, if they think one is called for, based on what they see with the little camera on the end of the tube they shove down my nose and throat to look at my innards. After they decide I'm stable enough to sit up, they allow me to sit in the waiting room with Gene while they figure out what they're going to tell me. Gene drove down from Bellingham to wait this out with me and take me home.

Today's procedure is five weeks after Gene's surgery. His recovery at my place was brief, only a week, and he was able to go back to his house and take care of himself.

I went to my appointment with the gastro doctor a few days after Gene's surgery. He said they need to take an even closer look … "It's probably nothing," he said when he told me that. I hate it when doctors say, "It's probably nothing." That usually means there is something, and it could be bad. So here we are awaiting the results of the biopsy.

"We drew some fluid from the cyst—that's what the lesion was—and we're going to have to send it to the lab for a biopsy. It'll take a few days to determine the outcome. We don't expect to find anything serious."

Yeah. Right. That's why they put me back under. That's why they're doing a biopsy. That's why a procedure that was supposed to take forty-five minutes took an hour and a half. Nothing serious. I'm screwed.

· · · · ·

So. What does one do to wait out cancer test results? Saturday, I rested, and on Sunday, I bought a couple of alpacas. That's right. Alpacas. Those cute little critters that are supposed to be a good investment. My daughter, Rebecca, and her husband, Mark, have a few acres north of Seattle and they began raising alpacas a couple of years ago. Once exposed to those delightful little animals, who can resist? I guess I plan to stick around a while. No use buying alpacas if one is not going to live long enough to take advantage of the investment potential.

Monday and Tuesday, I went to work at a client's office. On Tuesday, the phone rang about 4:30 p.m.

"This is Dr. Kimmey. We have your test results. The (something) in the fluid indicates the presence of a tumor inside the cyst. I recommend that you have surgery as soon as possible. I've called your doctor. Good luck."

Good luck? *Good luck?!?* What the … when does a doctor say "Good luck?" What kind of thing is that for a doctor to say? That's even worse than "It's probably nothing."

I have a business dinner to go to. I blurt out to a friend and colleague sitting next to me at the table, "I got a call about an hour ago. I flunked a biopsy."

"Where?" he asks.

"Pancreas," I reply.

"Oh, that's nasty," he says. "What's next?"

"He said surgery. It's operable. That's a good thing."

When I get home, there is a message from my primary physician, the one who said, "You sure opened a can of worms," in his office when we were discussing what the next step would be with the information the body scan delivered. His message tonight says he will wait in his office until I return his call. It's nine p.m., and he is indeed waiting. He's redeemed himself. He recommends a surgeon and says he'll call him to tell him to expect my call. So, the ball is rolling right along. I have no idea what I'm going to tell my family.

It's late August, and I've messed everything up. It's such a beautiful summer we're having! Gene recovered completely from his surgery and he's back at work. His time with me wasn't so bad. Nothing is ever as bad as dreaded expectations. So, he's fine. The girls are fine, and the grandkids are fine. And I have to mess it all up. What'll I tell them? I'm not going to tell them anything for a few days. I'm going to chew on this a while by myself.

I make my appointment with Dr. McLanahan to discuss the surgery. I'm going to take someone with me for the discussion. When Mom was ill, we found it helped significantly to have two sets of ears listening to the medical talk. It's hard for one person to take it all in. But I'm going to have to tell someone, soon. Piss.

I call my son-in-law, Mark. "Well, the biopsy didn't turn out the way we'd have liked. How am I going to tell Becca?"

"When you said they had to put you back under for more tests, we knew something was up. She's been waiting to hear the results. I'll tell her to take her cell phone outside to take your call."

"Hi. The biopsy results weren't so good. I'm going to have to have surgery. I'm seeing the surgeon next week."

"I didn't think it would be good news."

She's choked up, and we hang up. We need some time to gather this in.

Shannon called me. "I want to go with you to see the doctor."

Gene called. Since his surgery, he got himself a cell phone. "Do you want me to come down this weekend?"

"No. Next weekend is the Huskies' first home game."

"When are you going to see the doctor?"

"Next week."

Dr. McLanahan says he will do what is called Whipple Procedure. Basically, they take my abdominal insides out, look at it all, chop out a bunch of it, and put whatever looks good back in. I'll be in the hospital ten days to two weeks.

"This is the most complicated abdominal surgery we do."

"How many of these do you do?" Shannon asked.

"One a year."

• • • • •

"Sorry I asked," she says.

I'm sitting in Husky stadium next to Gene, and I look around. It's a gorgeous day and the Huskies are expected to win the game. I wonder if this is my last Huskies game. I look at the lake on the east end of the stadium. I look at the clouds coming from the west. I look at the people around me, and I look at my brother. Is this my last time in Husky stadium with my brother?

Screw that kind of thinking! If it is my last game, I sure as Hell won't know it. I'll be bug dust. That's what Dad said when he was headed for the Happy Hunting Ground. "I'll be bug dust soon," he said.

Well, I don't believe I'm ready to be bug dust. The crowd is "woofing." The Dawgs are about to score. "Woof, woof, woof!" Bug dust my ass.

All my paperwork is done so there's none of that left to take care of. It's Sunday night and three of us, Texie, Gene and I, are having dinner at Uptown China, all dressed up, of course. Tonight, it's chopsticks. Tomorrow it's a knife.

"What'll you have, ladies?" the waiter asks.

Gene orders for us. His deep voice causes a bit of a blink from the waiter. We look at each other and grin.

Gene says to me, "If you don't mind, I'm going to wear my lucky dress to the hospital tomorrow, the one I wore when I went in for my surgery. That turned out all right."

How could I possibly mind?

Chapter Twenty

ALL IS WELL
The banjo returns

After dinner I had two phone conversations that remain in my mind. The first was from a lifelong friend, Penny Smith, who almost became a sister when her Dad and my Mom dated several years ago. Gene and Penny also dated during one of the summers that Mom and George were dating.

Over the years, Penny discovered her true identity and "came out" without hesitation. She discovered that she is a lesbian. But I don't know her as "a lesbian." I know Penny as a successful career woman, a dear friend, and a sister. Now there's a twist. I actually have had a sister, for a long time. Penny is my first sister and Gene, in line of appearance, is my second sister. Penny and I are the kind of sisters I understand. We talk about our families, our careers, our present and future activities, and our dreams. We've visited each other in our homes many times. I have never seen her underwear.

Penny lives in Southern California. Tonight, she and I reminisce about our lifetime relationship, including my staying with her father, George, when Penny was in the hospital. She had a mastectomy to rid herself of breast cancer. We've shared much over the time we have known each other.

Both our parents are gone, and the two of us remain close. Penny lives the life of a well-rounded human being. Her sexuality is not an issue. It is just a part of who she is.

Oh, how I hope Gene can get to that point!

There is a bit of awkwardness when our conversation draws to a close. If what happens tomorrow is not good, our days as sisters on this earth could be over sooner rather than later. How do we say goodbye tonight? "It's been great … good luck … hope to see you again" … blah, blah, chuckle, click.

The other phone call came from another longtime friend. I won't mention her name. She called to ask me if I'd found Jesus. She's concerned. She doesn't know my religious leanings. She's worried I may go down the road to Hell sometime tomorrow.

Good Lord. Sorry. Bad choice of words. I don't think I'll be going down any such roads for a long time, if ever.

I hear I missed an adventure in the lobby of the hospital. Judith, another one of my friends who showed up to be on watch, admitted to being "startled" by my brother's appearance in his lucky dress, but she laughed as she told me about it. Apparently, there was a round of well-wishers throughout the day. I didn't see anyone other than Rebecca and Mark, who drove me to the hospital and walked me to the changing room. It was weird walking away from them in my surgical outfit. I felt very, very small. Much of my adventure commenced in what followed the eight-hour surgery.

September 18, 2002, was the date. On October 7, while I was still in the hospital, the nurses brought me my first solid food. They brought me a birthday cake, with a lighted candle. Nice to have a birthday, and even nicer to celebrate it with real food.

I went home October 14, with two tubes hanging out of my abdomen. It was a rough go at the hospital and it remains tough, but I am home with no traces of cancer; and no gall bladder, no duodenum, and only a small part of a pancreas. My small intestine has been stretched upward and attached to my stomach, etc, etc. I got a re-org of my digestive system. But they say the bad cells are all gone.

So we have two cancers struck down by one Lucky Dress? I've believed in goofier things.

Gene offered to stay and take care of me. I said no. I've taken care of myself for a lifetime. I couldn't handle someone hovering over me, or touching me. I'm still a privacy nut. I can't change at this stage of the game. We're way past half-time. This game plan cannot be altered.

We're unable to attend football games at the stadium this season, but Gene comes to see me on Husky weekends. We watch the game together on television, sitting on the sofa, Gene in a silky purple print dress, me in blue jeans and a purple T-shirt.

"New dress?"

"Yeah. I got it for Huskies games."

"Nice print."

Game over. Dawgs win.

Hey! Is that a banjo on his knee? Is that Foggy Mountain Breakdown I hear?

Gene looks at me over the top of his glasses and grins. Everything is "normal" again.

I wrote all about our surgeries and health issues to put on the table that there are more important issues than who wears what. In our earlier conversations, Gene said he believes that what we wear defines us. I'm not so sure I agree with that. What we wear is just window-dressing. Showing up, offering support, living and laughing together is what defines us. That is who we are. And I happen to like who we are. Life is good with my Brother/Sister. If he is wearing a dress and I am wearing the jeans, I can live with that.

Can you?

EPILOGUE

Our surgeries took place in 2002. We both recovered. We both beat the Big C. It had to have been Gene's lucky dress. It's the only explanation that makes sense.

Mom had to wait until July 2008 to have her son with her again. Gene died July 27, 2008, from complications of diabetes. Damn those deep-fried chicken gizzards!

He got to live nearly fourteen years as his "real" self, in the company of friends and family. We all became comfortable with the many facets of the person he was.

And we all miss him very much.

About the Author
Shirleyanne Thom

Shirleyanne Thom, professionally known as Shirley Thom, was a Home Economics major at Colorado Women's College. With an Associate Degree in hand, she married her childhood sweetheart and gave birth to two daughters. Fortunately, she also attended a secretarial school. When their daughters were five and eight years old, Shirleyanne's husband decided he no longer wanted to be married with family responsibilities. She needed to find a job.

She was hired as a receptionist for a local radio station and worked her way into sales and management positions. Shirley Thom expanded her skills to include professional marketing and media negotiation, and is now self-employed, specializing in sports and entertainment events.

Along the way, Shirleyanne also wrote four books, drawn from personal experiences: the first and second editions of *Life Is a Sales Job*, written to encourage people to consider careers in commissioned sales; *Promise, I'll Stay for Mother's Day*, a personal memoir that traces the changing roles of women inside and outside the family, from 1906 through 2006; and now *She's My Brother*, the story of her brother, Gene Wilson, who lived a lonely life as a cross-dresser, from age four to fifty-four, when he finally "came out" to his sister, Shirleyanne.

This book is about family secrets and societal taboos, and how they influence our personal and professional lives.

SHE'S MY BROTHER
And I Miss Him

DISCOVERING A CROSS-DRESSER:
BETTER LATE THAN NEVER?

In this honest, heartrending account by a loving sister, family secrets, social taboos, and self-acceptance all come into play.

From the age of four, Gene harbored a secret desire to wear his sister's clothes—not the wardrobe he was expected to wear as a little boy. He wanted to be Shirleyanne's sister—not her brother. Back then, negative social attitudes forced cross-dressers to hide their secret even from family. But when Gene's parents made what was to them an embarrassing discovery, they kept their daughter Shirleyanne in the dark.

It took a serious illness 50 years later to bring out the truth and open emotional wounds that needed special perception, understanding, acceptance—and, finally, love to heal.

"My brother lived a long, lonely life before he 'came out,'" says the author, "but he wanted his story told. I'm not sure I understand the complexities of cross-dressing, but I understand more than I did. I am sharing our story because I hope our personal journey will bring about a greater appreciation for the vastness and varieties of the human race. We are all a part of it, and we are worth the effort it will take for us humans to learn to live better together."

· · · · ·

"An emotional roller coaster between a brother and sister that opens our eyes to a not-uncommon scenario."

MEMOIR

Published by
EDK Books

Distributed by
EDK Distribution, LLC

$14.95
ISBN 978-1-7339618-8-2
51495>

9 781733 961882